Winning and Losing

Studies in Joshua, Judges, and Ruth

R.E. Harlow

Everyday Publications Inc.
310 Killaly Street W.
Port Colborne, ON   L3K 6A6
Canada

WINNING AND LOSING

God led Israel out of Egypt and into the land of Palestine. At first the people won victories but when they sinned their enemies won the battle.

In the book of Joshua, Israel was winning battles most of the time. In the book of Judges, Israel was losing battles most of the time.

We Christians are often the same. God wants us to win in the spiritual battle but too often we lose because we do not trust Him fully.

One thing that will help you win spiritual battles is to read the Bible every day. This book will help you understand God's Word.

On pages 4 and 5 you will see which verses to read each day. For example, on the first day of the first month, read the first chapter of Joshua, verses 1 to 9 (Joshua 1:1-9). On page 9, you will see a little number on the left side. The number 1/1 means that you start here on the first day of the first month. On page 11, number 1/2 shows what you should read on the second day.

Some days you will have questions to answer. Try to answer these questions first without looking back at the Bible or this book. If you are not sure, you may look back.

This plan will help you to read through Joshua, Judges, and Ruth in six months. You can start whenever you like but be sure to keep up by reading a little bit every day. God will help you to understand His precious Word.

Copyright © 1967 by R.E. Harlow
ISBN 978-0-919586-04-8
Revised edition 2005
Cover design by Della Letkeman
Photo Courtesy of Todd Bolen/bibleplaces.com

Printed in Canada

Studies in Joshua, Judges, and Ruth

Joshua

Judges

Ruth

READ THE BIBLE EVERY DAY

	First Month	Second Month	Third Month
1	Joshua 1:1- 9	10:24-33	19:49-51
2	1:10-18	10:34-43	20:1- 6
3	2:1-7	11:1- 8	20:7- 9
4	2:8-16	11:9-14	21:1- 3
5	2:17-24	11:15-23	21:4- 8
6	3:1-6	12:1- 8	21:9-19
7	3:7-17	12:9-24	21:20-26
8	4:1-10	13:1- 7	21:27-33
9	4:11-18	13:8-13	21:34-40
10	4:19-24	13:14-23	21:41-45
11	5:1- 9	13:24-28	22:1- 6
12	5:10-15	13:29-33	22:7-14
13	6:1- 8	14:1-5	22:15-20
14	6:9-19	14. 6-15	22:21-29
15	6:20-27	15:1-12	22:30-34
16	7:1- 8	15:13-19	23:1- 13
17	7:9-15	15:20-44	23:14 -16
18	7:16-26	15:45-63	24:1- 7
19	8:1- 8	16:1-10	24:8-13
20	8:9-13	17:1-6	24:14-21
21	8:14-23	17:7-13	24:22-28
22	8:24-29	17:14-18	24:29-33
23	8:30-35	18:1-10	Frames 1- 4
24	9:1- 6	18:11-28	5- 8
25	9:7-15	19:1- 9	9-12
26	9:16-21	19:10-16	13-16
27	9:22-27	19:17-23	17-20
28	10:1- 7	19:24-31	Judges 1:1-7
29	10:8-14	19:32-39	1:8-15
30	10:15-23	19:40-48	1:16-21

READ THE BIBLE EVERY DAY

	Fourth Month		Fifth Month		Sixth Month
1	Judges 1:22-29		9:30-38		18:21-31
2	1:30-36		9:39-49		19:1- 9
3	2:1- 5		9:50-57		19:10-21
4	2:6-15		10:1- 9		19:22-30
5	2:16-23		10:10-18		20:1- 7
6	3:1-6		11:1-11		20:8-18
7	3:7-13		11:12-17		20:19-28
8	3:14-23		11:18-23		20:29-36
9	3:24-31		11:24-30		20:37-48
10	4:1-10		11:31-33		21:1- 7
11	4:11-16		11:34-40		21:8-12
12	4:17-24		12:1- 7		21:13-15
13	5:1-5		12:8-15		21:16-25
14	5:6-12		13:1- 7		Ruth 1:1- 7
15	5:13-22		13:8-14		1:8-14
16	5:23-31		13:15-25		1:15-22
17	6:1-10		14:1- 7		2:1- 7
18	6:11-14		14:8-14		2:8-16
19	6:15-24		14:15-20		2:17-23
20	6:25-32		15:1- 8		3:1- 5
21	6:33-40		15:9-13		3:6-13
22	7:1-8		15:14-20		3:14-18
23	7:9-18		16:1- 9		4:1- 6
24	7:19-25		16:10-14		4:7-12
25	8:1-12		16:15-22		4:13-22
26	8:13-21		16:23-31		Frames 1- 2
27	8:22-35		17:1- 6		3- 6
28	9:1- 6		17:7-13		7-10
29	9:7-21		18:1-10		11-16
30	9:22-29		18:11-20		17-22

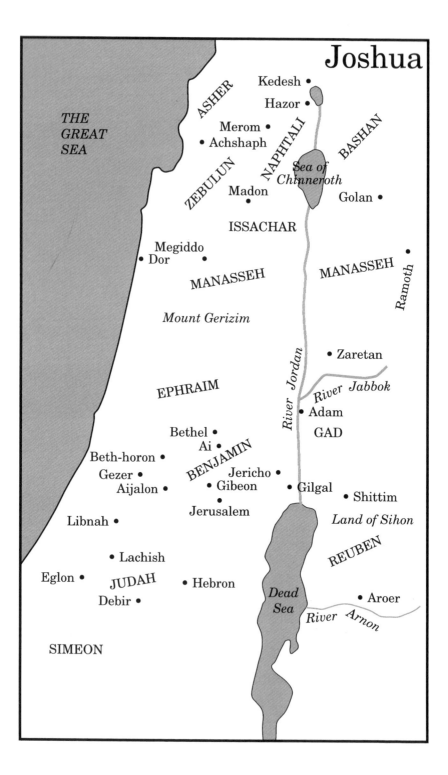

Joshua

THE
GREAT
SEA

ASHER

Kedesh •

Hazor •

Merom •
• Achshaph

NAPHTALI

BASHAN

ZEBULUN

Sea of
Chinneroth

Madon •

Golan •

ISSACHAR

Megiddo
• Dor   •

MANASSEH

MANASSEH

Ramoth •

Mount Gerizim

EPHRAIM

River Jordan

• Zaretan

River Jabbok

• Adam

GAD

Bethel •

Ai •

Beth-horon •

BENJAMIN

Gezer •

Jericho •

Aijalon •

• Gibeon

• Gilgal

• Shittim

Jerusalem •

Land of Sihon

Libnah •

REUBEN

• Lachish

Eglon •

JUDAH

• Hebron

Dead
Sea

• Aroer

Debir •

River Arnon

SIMEON

1 THE ISRAELITES ENTER THE LAND

The first five books of the Bible are called the Law or the Books of Moses. We do not know who wrote Joshua, Judges, Samuel, and Kings, but the Jews called these books the *Early Prophets*. These books tell the story of the people of Israel, and, together with Ruth and the next five books (1 and 2 Chronicles, Ezra, Nehemiah, Esther) can be called the *Historical Books*.

The first book in the Bible, Genesis, tells us that in the beginning God created the heavens and the earth. Adam fell into sin and all his children were born with a sinful nature and followed his example. They sinned greatly against the Lord and He destroyed them all except Noah and his family. However Noah's descendants continued to sin against the Lord. At last God called out one man, Abraham, and promised to bless him. The second part of Genesis tells the story of Abraham, Isaac, Jacob, and Joseph.

Joseph became a ruler in Egypt, next to the king himself. After Joseph's death another king made the people of Israel into slaves and for many years they had to work very hard without receiving any salary. God raised up Moses to save His people and bring them to the land which He had promised to Abraham. The book of Exodus tells us that God brought Israel out of Egypt and commanded them to build the tabernacle. Leviticus teaches us how the people could approach God with sacrifices. In Numbers we read about their journey through the desert to Canaan, the land of promise. In Deuteronomy Moses reminded Israel of all the commands God had given them and told them to obey the Lord and His Law.

In the book of Joshua we see that Israel entered Canaan. But after Joshua died the people fell into sin and their enemies defeated them. The book of Judges shows that God raised up men to deliver Israel from their enemies. However after a while many people went back into sin, but even so there were some people in Israel who still followed the Lord. Ruth was one of these. She was a woman of Moab but had come to know and love the God of Israel and to live with His people.

The books of Samuel tell us about Samuel the prophet, Saul the first king of Israel, and King David. In the two books of Kings we read about the rule of Solomon, the division of the kingdom of Israel during the rule of his son Rehoboam, and the kings of Israel and Judah who followed him. In all these books the people continued to live in sin. Finally God punished them by allowing their enemies to defeat them and to take them as prisoners to Babylon.

The books of Chronicles repeat the history of Israel from the time of King David until the people were carried away as prisoners to another land. The people of Israel repented of their sins while they were prisoners in Babylon and God opened the way for them to return to their land. Ezra and Nehemiah told about this in their books. Esther did not return to Israel but served the Lord as the wife of the king of Persia.

All these books have important lessons for us today. Let us consider first the life of Joshua and the teaching contained in the book which is called by his name.

The last chapter of Deuteronomy tells us that Moses died, but at that time the people of Israel were still not in the land of Canaan. The people were filled with great sorrow when Moses died and they did not know what they should do next. They did not need to worry because the Lord had already prepared another leader for them. This was Joshua to whom God spoke in the first verse of this book.

Who was Joshua? He was the son of Nun, of the tribe of Ephraim, Numbers 13:8, and was born when the Israelites were still in Egypt, Numbers 32:11,12. His grandfather was the leader of Ephraim, 1 Chronicles 7:26,27; Numbers 1:10.

We first read about Joshua as a soldier. Moses commanded him to choose men and go out to fight against the people of Amalek. At the same time, Moses, Aaron, and Hur went to the top of the hill. The soldiers of Israel were stronger than those of Amalek as long as Moses held up his hands, Exodus 17:11, so Joshua learned early in his life that God gives the victory in answer to prayer. The Lord had already chosen Joshua to be a leader in Israel and was preparing him for this work, Exodus 17:14.

Joshua became Moses' helper and went up Mount Sinai with him at the time God told Moses how to build the tabernacle, Exodus 24:13; 25:8,9. Moses and Joshua were on the mountain for forty days and nights, and during that time the people of Israel fell into terrible sin. Moses and Joshua heard a noise in the camp of Israel as they were coming down the mountain. Joshua thought it was the noise of people making war, but Moses recognized it as the sound of people singing, Exodus 32:15-18.

At this time Joshua was a young man who had a real desire to be close to the Lord, Exodus 33:11, but he still had lessons to learn. For example, he had to learn that he should not be jealous when the Lord blessed and used other people, Numbers 11:26-29. He also learned to do what was right even when most other people did what was wrong. Moses sent twelve men to look over the land of Canaan. Ten of these men brought back the report that the people in Canaan were too strong for Israel. The other two, Joshua and Caleb, believed that God would help Israel to defeat them, Numbers 14:6-8. As a result the people of Israel refused to go into Canaan even though God had promised to give it to them. God judged all Israel because they did not believe in Him, and He said that all of them would die in the desert except Caleb and Joshua, Numbers 26:65. The Lord showed that He had chosen Joshua to be the leader of Israel after Moses died, and He put His spirit on him, Numbers 27:18-21; Deuteronomy 31:7,8,14,23.

Joshua himself may have written the book of Joshua, 24:16. Both Stephen and the writer of Hebrews knew that the history of this book was true, Acts 7:45; Hebrews 4:8; 11:30. God gave Joshua a wonderful promise, Joshua 1:5, a promise which is given to all of us by the Holy Spirit, Hebrews 13:5. Rahab is mentioned in the New Testament, see Hebrews 11:31 and James 2:25. We can be sure that God has given us the book of Joshua and that it teaches us the truth.

GOD COMMANDED ISRAEL TO ENTER THE LAND,

chapter 1

1/1   Moses died after leading the people of Israel for forty years. Yes, their leader was dead, but God commanded His people to go forward just the same. God's servants may leave this world but God's work must continue. This work can be compared to building a house. Many people share in the work of putting up a house. Different people do different types of work, but it is all done according to the plan of the builder. Christians are also putting up a spiritual building, 1 Corinthians 3:10,11; Ephesians 2:20-22, and they must all build according to God's plan so that the building will be as He wants it. Some of the workmen die when their work here on earth is finished, but others keep on doing God's work according to the plan He has given us in Scripture.

God told Joshua to be courageous, 1:1-9

Moses was dead and now God commanded Joshua to lead the people of Israel across the Jordan River and into the land of Canaan, 1:1,2. He promised Joshua that all the land belonged to them and that they would be able to defeat all their enemies because God was with them, 1:3-6.

God gave Israel the whole land of Canaan, but for many years they did not possess it all. In verse 3 we see that only the land on which they walked would really be theirs. The books of Joshua and Judges show that Israel did not get the complete victory over the people of the land.

This is an important lesson for us. God has blessed us with every spiritual blessing in Christ, Ephesians 1:3, but there are many Christians who do not gain the victory over sin and do not have joy and peace in their hearts because they do not really believe God's promises.

God commanded Joshua to be brave and to obey the Law of Moses. We too need courage to obey God's commands because often people laugh at those who say they are Christians.

God also told Joshua to think about the Word of God day and night, and promised him that he would succeed if he obeyed this command.

These promises are for Christians today as well. The Lord promises us success in our service for Him if we do it according to the instructions given in His Word. He promises to be with us and He will never fail us, 1:5; Hebrews 13:5. All we have to do is to trust and obey Him.

Joshua told the people to enter the land, 1:10-18

1/2   Joshua heard the Lord's command to lead the people into the land of Canaan and he called the officers at once. He commanded them to tell the people to prepare food for the journey so that they would be able to leave in three days, 1:10,11.

Joshua had to give a special command to two and a half of the twelve tribes. The tribes of Reuben, Gad, and half the tribe of Manasseh had decided before that they would rather live outside the land of promise on the east of the river Jordan. They chose this land because they thought it would be good for their cattle, Numbers 32:1-5.

Many years before this, Lot chose to leave Abraham for the same reason and he went to live in the valley of Jordan. He left the place of God's blessing in order to become richer in this world, but at the end of his life he did not have either riches or the blessing of the Lord, Genesis 19.

Moses had agreed to let the two and a half tribes remain east of the Jordan River if they promised to help the other tribes fight for their land, Numbers 32:17,20-22. So the Lord allowed the two and a half tribes to live in the land east of Jordan, 1:12,13, although He really wanted them to live in the land of Canaan together with the other tribes. The men of the tribes of Reuben, Gad, and Manasseh agreed to obey Joshua as they had obeyed Moses, 1:16,17.

The true servant of the Lord does not make his own plans and then ask the Lord to bless them. We should ask the Lord to show us what *His* will is and obey all His commands. These men said they would kill anyone who did not obey the commands of Joshua, but they themselves had not really tried to do God's will.

In this chapter Moses is called *the servant* of the Lord five times, and in the rest of the book, thirteen times more. It is a great honor to be called the servant of the Lord. The Bible described Joshua in the same way after he died, Joshua 24:29; Judges 2:8. The Lord Jesus Christ was also called the Servant of Jehovah, Matthew 12:18; Philippians 2:7. The Lord will give great honor to some Christians in heaven by calling them *good and faithful servants*, Matthew 25:21,23. These will have the joy of serving Him for ever.

RAHAB, chapter 2

1/3   At this time the people of Israel were still living in the land of
Moab near the city of Shittim, Numbers 22:1; 33:49. There the
false prophet Balaam had tried to bring evil on Israel. God had promised
to bless His people, but instead He had to punish them when they fell
into sin, Numbers 25:1. Moses had spoken to all Israel on the east side
of Jordan and had given the great messages of Deuteronomy,
Deuteronomy 1:1.

Rahab helped the men of Israel, 2:1-7

From Shittim Joshua sent two men to look over the city of
Jericho. No doubt he remembered the time forty years earlier when
Moses had sent him and Caleb and ten other men to look over the land
of Canaan, Numbers 13.

Joshua sent these two men secretly, but the king of Jericho heard
about it. The two men entered the house of Rahab, an immoral woman
who was living a sinful life, but who now wanted to worship the God of
Israel, Hebrews 11:31. Rahab told the men that all the people of Jericho
knew what Israel had done to two kings on the other side of Jordan and
that they were very much afraid.

Rahab sent the men away, 2:8-21

1/4   Rahab really believed in the God of Israel and she showed her
faith by what she did, that is by helping the men of Israel to get
away safely, James 2:25.

We can be saved only by faith in the Lord Jesus Christ, but
we must show our faith to others by doing good works, Titus
3:5; James 2:17.

Rahab had a great desire to save her family and this also showed
that she had really believed in God, 2:12,13. She was like another sinful
woman who believed in Christ, and at once wanted to bring others to
Him, John 4:28,29. Rahab asked the men to promise that the people of
Israel would save her father's family when they came to take the city.
The men agreed to do this if she helped them to escape, but if they were
caught and killed, Israel would take the city of Jericho and Rahab would
also be killed. They told Rahab to tie a red cord in her window and to

bring all the members of her family into the house because everyone inside the house would be safe. Perhaps the men were thinking of the blood on the door which saved the oldest son in each family in Israel when they were still in Egypt, Exodus 12:23.

1/5   Perhaps you wonder why God would save an immoral woman like Rahab. It is true that Rahab was a very sinful woman, but the Lord Jesus came to save sinners, not righteous people, Luke 5:32. Both heaven and hell will be full of sinners, but those in heaven are the ones who have repented of their sins and have believed in the Lord Jesus Christ.

You may also wonder why Rahab told a lie about the men she was trying to help. The Bible does not say that she did what was right, and in Revelation 21:8 we see that liars of every kind will be judged. Some people believe in Christ after they have lived in sin for many years and it is hard for them to break those sinful habits right away, but God has promised to give them the victory.

The two men returned to Joshua, 2:22-24

The men hid in the hills for three days and then returned to Joshua. They told him that the people of Jericho were very afraid of Israel. Their report gave Joshua still more courage.

THE PEOPLE OF ISRAEL CROSSED THE JORDAN RIVER,
chapters 3,4

1/6   No doubt the people of Canaan felt that the river Jordan would make it hard for any army to attack them from that direction, especially at that time of year when the water was very high in the river, 3:15. Even so the Canaanites were afraid because they had heard that the Lord had dried up the water of the Red Sea for the people of Israel, 2:10.

In faith Israel prepared to cross the Jordan, 3:1-6

Three days had passed since Joshua had told the people of Israel to get ready for the journey, 1:11; 2:22, and now the people moved from

Shittim to the edge of the Jordan. After three more days the officers told the people to follow the Ark of the Lord. The Ark was a box made of wood and covered with gold. It contained the stones on which the Law had been written. The Lord had commanded that only Kohathites should carry the Ark, Exodus 25:10,11; Numbers 4:15. The people had always followed the Ark as they traveled through the desert, Numbers 10:33. Now the priests had to carry the Ark and the people were to stay about 3000 feet (900 meters) behind it, 3:3,4.

The presence of God is very holy, and that is the reason the Israelites had to stay so far away from the Ark. However today Christians can enter into the Most Holy Place because of the death of the Lord Jesus Christ, Hebrews 10:19. We should walk close to the Lord and not far behind as Peter did, Mark 14:54. We too can say every day as we are on our way to heaven that we have not traveled this way before, 3:4. Each day we need the Lord to guide us and He has promised to do so, Psalm 32:8.

Then Joshua commanded the people to make themselves pure and holy because the Lord would do a great miracle among them the next day, 3:5. God wanted the people to be clean from their sins. Perhaps we see so little blessing in the work of the Lord today because of sin in the lives of Christians, 2 Timothy 2:21.

The next day Joshua commanded the priests to lift the Ark and to go ahead of the people, 3:6, but Joshua himself did not know yet just what the Lord would do for them.

The Lord strengthened Israel's faith, 3:7-13

1/7   Now Jehovah told Joshua that He would give him great honor in the eyes of the people of Israel. He told Joshua to command the priests to go and stand with the Ark in the water near the edge of the river, 3:7,8. Joshua repeated the Lord's words to the people. God was going to do a miracle to help them believe that He would give them the victory over all their enemies in the land of Canaan. God told them that the water of the river would be stopped so that they would be able to get across to the other side. He also told them to choose a man from each tribe for a special work, 3:12. We will see in the next chapter, verses 4-8, what this work was.

The people obeyed and God honored their faith, 3:14-17

Note that God had spoken to Joshua and Joshua had told the people the Lord's words. They obeyed the Lord's command and walked to the Jordan. The water continued to flow in the river until the feet of the priests were actually in the water. Then the water piled up at the city of Adam about 15 miles (24 kilometers) north of Jericho and the river bed dried up. The priests stood on dry ground while all the people went across to the other side.

This is the way the Lord teaches us to have faith. We believe and obey His Word and take one step forward in little faith. Then we see the Lord working for us and our faith is strengthened. We are now ready to believe and obey when He tells us to do something more difficult and for which we need more faith.

Stones to help the people remember, 4:1-10

1/8　All the people had now crossed the river and the Lord told Joshua to speak to the twelve men whom he had chosen. Each man should take a stone from the center of the river where the priests were standing, and carry it to the other side, 4:1-3. Joshua told the men to do as the Lord had commanded and he explained to them the reason for this command. Later on the children of the people of Israel would ask about the meaning of these stones, and their fathers would be able to tell them about the time when the Lord made a way for them through the Jordan River, 4:4-7.

No doubt the children of the people of Israel also asked their fathers about the Passover, Exodus 12:26; about killing or redeeming the firstborn animal, Exodus 13:13,14; and about the laws of Jehovah, Deuteronomy 6:20. Their fathers were to be prepared to answer them and to tell them about the goodness and power of Jehovah. Today Christians should also teach their children about the Lord, Ephesians 6:4.

The men picked up the twelve stones and piled them up at Gilgal on the west side of Jordan. God thought of the nation of Israel as one nation even though two and a half tribes wanted to stay on the east side of the river, separated from the rest of the nation. Joshua also set up twelve stones in the middle of the Jordan which were soon covered with water.

The Jordan River speaks of death and these twelve stones are a picture of believers. We are crucified with Christ, Galatians 2:20, and are dead with Christ, Romans 6:8; 2 Corinthians 5:14. Today we are alive so that we might live for the glory of God.

The priests crossed the river, 4:11-18

1/9   Only 40,000 men of the tribes of Reuben and Gad and the half tribe of Manasseh crossed over Jordan to help the other tribes fight their enemies. There were 43,730 men in the tribe of Reuben, 40,500 in the tribe of Gad, and 52,700 in Manasseh at the time Moses numbered the people. Perhaps half the men of the tribe of Manasseh had decided to stay on the east side of Jordan. If so, 110,580 men should have crossed over to help their brothers, Numbers 26:7,18,34. Joshua had commanded all the men of war to come across and help the other tribes and they had agreed to do so, 1:14,16, but they did not keep their promise. Do we always keep our promises?

Reuben	43,730
Gad	40,500
Half of Manasseh	26,350
Total	110,580

At last the priests also crossed over, and as soon as they had come out of the river the waters started to flow again. The people had great respect for Joshua as a result of this miracle, 4:14.

The people camped in Gilgal, 4:19-24

1/10   These things took place only about a month after Moses' death (see Deuteronomy 1:3 and *Desert Journey*, page 87–a study of Numbers and Deuteronomy, from EVERYDAY PUBLICATIONS). The people now camped in Gilgal. Later their children would ask about the pile of stones and they should tell them about God's great power which made it possible for them to cross the Jordan River. In this way all people on earth would know that God has all power, and they would fear Him for ever, 4:24.

Even in Old Testament times God wanted the people of Israel to tell other nations about their great God.

Now Christ has risen from the dead and has commanded us to preach the Gospel to the people of every nation, Matthew 28:18-20; Mark 16:15,16. We are alive today in order that we may obey this command and tell others about our wonderful Savior.

TEST YOURSELF (Joshua 1-4)

1. What happened to the people of Israel before Joshua became their leader?

2. Where was Joshua born and what tribe did he belong to?

3. What did Joshua learn early in life?

4. Why did Joshua have to be brave?

5. Why did 2½ tribes choose to live outside the land God had promised to Israel?

6. How did Rahab show that she had real faith in Jehovah?

7. Why did Rahab tell a lie?

8. Why did Joshua tell the people to make themselves pure and holy?

9. When did the river Jordan stop flowing?

10. Why did Israel pile up twelve stones on the west side of Jordan?

11. Did the 2½ tribes keep their promise to help the others fight in Canaan?

Turn to page 112 to check your answers.

2 JERICHO AND AI

1/11　We have seen that Joshua led the people of Israel across Jordan into Canaan, the land of promise. God held back the water of Jordan so that they were able to cross over the river. As a result of this wonderful miracle the people knew God had made Joshua their leader in the place of Moses and that He would give them victory over all the nations of the land. The people of Canaan became very afraid when they heard about the miracle, but even so Israel had to go forward and defeat them.

THE WALLS OF JERICHO, chapters 5,6

The kings of the Amorites and of the Canaanites soon heard that the people of Israel had crossed over the Jordan River and were already in their land. They were very much afraid because they knew that Jehovah was with Israel, 5:1, but they decided to fight against Israel. How foolish to try and fight against Almighty God!

The people of Israel were not yet ready to fight and defeat their enemies. First, the Lord commanded Joshua to circumcise all the men, 5:2. Joshua prepared sharp knives and did as the Lord commanded.

God first commanded Abraham to be circumcised himself and to circumcise all the men of his household, Genesis 17:10-14. Circumcision was a sign of God's covenant with His people. Fathers in Israel circumcised their sons eight days after they were born. Moses had neglected to do this with his sons and God could not use him to deliver Israel until he did, Exodus 4:24-26.

All the men who had left Egypt had been circumcised but they did not circumcise their sons who were born while they journeyed through the desert. All these older men except Caleb and Joshua died before Israel entered Canaan because they had refused to obey God's command to enter the land, Numbers 14:29,30. Their hearts were not right with the Lord and this was no doubt the reason why they did not circumcise their sons.

The people of Israel had to obey God's command and be circumcised before they could enjoy God's blessing. Many Christians seem to think that they can choose whether they are going to obey God's commands or not. Circumcision may speak to us of baptism. Some Christians have never been baptized since they believed in Christ, but they cannot experience the blessing and victory which God wants to give them until they realize that they have been crucified with Christ, Galatians 2:19,20, and obey the command to be buried with Christ in baptism, Matthew 28:19; Romans 6:4.

Gilgal means "rolling". Before they were circumcised, the Israelites were like the Egyptians, but here at Gilgal the Lord *rolled* away the shame of Egypt from them. It is a shame for a Christian to be no different from the people of the world. Has the Lord commanded you to do something and you have not obeyed? You cannot expect Him to bless you until you get back to "Gilgal" and start obeying Him again.

In the New Testament we learn that people do not need to be circumcised in order to be saved and that circumcision is of no help to a Christian, Galatians 5:2-6. It is a picture of people who have set themselves wholly apart for God, Romans 2:29; Colossians 2:11.

1/12 The people of Israel kept the Passover four days after they crossed the Jordan River, 5:10. God had commanded Israel to keep the Passover every year on the fourteenth day of the first month. This was to remind them of the wonderful way in which God had brought them out of Egypt. They had obeyed this command in the second year after they left Egypt, Numbers 9:1-5, but we do not read that they did it again during their entire journey through the desert. At the end of 40 years in the desert Moses told them to keep the Passover, but he did not say that they had not been doing this each year, Deuteronomy 16:1.

The Israelites in the Old Testament were commanded by the Law of Moses to keep these feasts and holy days, but Christians today are no longer under the Law. Paul knew that some of the believers were keeping certain days as holy and he was afraid they were going back to the Law in order to obtain salvation, Galatians 4:10. Christians do meet together on the first day of the week to worship the Lord but they do not do this in order to obtain salvation or to help them get to heaven. All we need in order to obtain eternal life is to believe in Christ, our Passover Lamb who died for us, 1 Corinthians 5:7; John 3:36.

The day after the Passover the people of Israel ate the ordinary food of the land, 5:11,12. God had provided manna from heaven as their food from the day they left Egypt for the whole forty years that they journeyed through the desert, Exodus 16:15,35. Now the long journey was over and God would no longer send the manna because in the land of Canaan they would be able to buy food or work for it by planting it themselves. It is God's will that men should work for their food, 2 Thessalonians 3:10-12.

The manna, the bread from heaven, is a picture of the Lord Jesus Christ, the Bread of Life, John 6:48-51. The Lord Jesus Christ will never fail us, and at the end of our long journey through this world He will welcome us to His home for ever, John 14:2,3.

Now the people were ready to fight against the men of Jericho. The Lord appeared to Joshua in the form of a man with a sword in his hand and told him just what they should do in order to take the city, 5:13-15. Joshua saw this man and, like a good soldier, he went to see if he was a friend or an enemy. The Lord certainly was not on the side of the enemies of Israel and He was not just a helper of Israel either. So He told Joshua that He was the Captain of the army of the Lord, 5:14. Joshua fell down on his face and worshiped the Lord and asked what He wanted him to do. The Lord told Joshua first to take off his shoes because the presence of Jehovah made even the ground holy, 5:15. Many years before Moses took off his shoes when the Lord appeared to him, Exodus 3:5; Acts 7:33.

1/13   Joshua took off his shoes, listened to the commands of the Lord and passed them on to the people, 6:1-7. The people of Jericho had closed the gates of their city and no one could come into the city or go out. The city was surrounded by high walls with strong gates. Even so Jehovah told Joshua that He had given the city to Israel. God would make the walls of the city fall down and Israel would kill the men of Jericho. First all the soldiers had to walk around the city once a day for six days with seven priests blowing seven trumpets going behind them. These priests were followed by others who carried the Ark of Jehovah, and behind them, by the rest of the people. Previously the priests carrying the Ark had gone ahead of all the other people as they traveled through the desert, but now God changed that order.

1/14   At first Joshua did not tell the people that the wall of Jericho would fall down. He commanded seven of the priests to blow their trumpets and the rest of them to carry the Ark, 6:6. He told the soldiers to go around the city in front of the priests and the other people to follow the priests. They had to do this without saying a word, 6:10. Israel walked around the city of Jericho in this way for six days, a distance of perhaps a mile or two (2 or 3 kilometers) which would take them less than an hour.

On the seventh day they marched around the city seven times. Joshua now told the people that the Lord had given them the city and that they had to kill all the people in the city except Rahab and her family who were in the house with her. They had to destroy everything in the city except things made of metal, 6:16-19. These belonged to the Lord. At Joshua's command the people gave a shout and the walls of the city fell down flat. The Israelite soldiers walked straight forward into the city and killed the people and all the animals in the city.

1/15   Joshua called the two men whom he had sent before to look over the city and told them to bring out Rahab and those who were with her, 6:22. The people also took everything made of metal and brought it to the Lord, 6:24.

Rahab and her family lived among the people of Israel until the time the book of Joshua was written, 6:25. She married Salmon, a man of the tribe of Judah. One of their sons was Boaz, the grandfather of Jesse, the father of King David, Matthew 1:5,6. Rahab believed in God and had shown her faith by saving the two men whom Joshua had sent. No doubt she could have escaped to some other land when the people of Israel came to take the city, but she chose to live with the people of God. She became an ancestor of David and also of the Lord Jesus Christ.

God had commanded Israel to destroy the city of Jericho because the people of that city were very evil. The people obeyed this command and Joshua put a curse on any man who attempted to build the city again. No one who feared the Lord would try to do so because of this curse. In the days of wicked King Ahab a man did build Jericho again and he and his family were judged by God, 1 Kings 16:34. The people in all the land of Canaan heard about Joshua and knew that the Lord was with him, 6:27.

THE SIN OF ACHAN, chapter 7

1/16   Are you enjoying victory or blessing in your own life or in your church? Then be especially careful because Satan is always ready to attack us when we have too much confidence in ourselves.

Israel had crossed over Jordan and the walls of the city had fallen down flat, but now God was angry with Israel, 7:1. At first Joshua did not know the reason for His anger, because he did not know that there was sin among the people of Israel.

Achan belonged to the tribe of Judah, one of the more important tribes of Israel. He had disobeyed God's command by taking something from Jericho for himself. Achan was an Israelite and God was angry with the whole nation because of the sin of this one man.

Joshua did not know what Achan had done and did not realize that the Lord was angry with Israel. He sent men to look over the next town, Ai, and these men found that only a few soldiers would be needed to destroy this city. So Joshua sent only 3000 men to take the city, but the Lord was not with them and the men of Ai were stronger than the Israelite soldiers and killed thirty-six of them.

The people of Israel became very much afraid when they saw this, 7:2-5. Joshua and the elders tore their clothes. They lay on the ground face down before the Ark of the Lord until evening, and threw dust on their heads, 7:6. Joshua asked the Lord why He had brought Israel across the Jordan River in order to destroy them. It would have been better for them to stay on the other side of the river. Joshua seemed to realize that he should not speak to God like this but he did not know what else to say, 7:8. He was really afraid that the people of Canaan would destroy Israel and that this would bring shame on the name of Jehovah, 7:9.

1/17   The Lord answered Joshua's prayer found in verse 9; this was more pleasing to Him than his prayer in verse 7. He told Joshua why the Israelites had been defeated, 7:10-12. They had disobeyed

God's command by taking for themselves what should have been burnt in Jericho and by stealing what belonged to Jehovah, 7:11. Only one man had done these things, perhaps with the help of his family, but God looked on the nation as one.

The sin of one man always harms many other people. We do not read that Achan told a lie with his lips, but he *acted* a lie which is even worse.

So God was angry with the whole nation because one man had taken for himself what should have been destroyed, 7:12. The Lord told Joshua to prepare the people because the next day He would make known which tribe was guilty, which family of that tribe, and which household of that family. Finally He would show who the guilty man was. God commanded that this man should be burned with fire together with all that belonged to him.

1/18   Early next morning God showed who the guilty person was. It was Achan, of the household of Zabdi, in the family of the Zarhites, of the tribe of Judah. Joshua asked Achan what he had done and Achan confessed that he had taken a beautiful garment that came from Shinar or Babylon, and some silver and gold. He had hidden these things in the ground under his tent, 7:20,21.

Joshua sent some men to Achan's tent. These men found that Achan had told the truth. So they took Achan to the valley of Achor, together with his family, the things he had stolen, and everything else that belonged to him, 7:22-26. There they stoned them with stones, burned them with fire, and covered their dead bodies with a great pile of stones. After that God was no longer angry with Israel, but the place was called "the valley of trouble."

What lessons does this sad chapter teach us? Achan said that he saw something with his eyes, wanted it for himself and then took it. The New Testament tells us that to want something you do not have is like worshiping idols, Ephesians 5:5; Colossians 3:5. We should keep ourselves from idols, 1 John 5:21, and be satisfied with what we have,

Hebrews 13:5. Loving money may lead you into all kinds of evil, 1 Timothy 6:10.

Achan thought he could hide his sin but God knew all about it, and the whole nation was guilty because of it. Of course we cannot hide anything from God. You hurt the whole church if you, a Christian, go on in sin. This is the reason many churches see so little blessing.

Perhaps the greatest lesson of this chapter is that sin always results in sorrow. It always makes God angry, and this is a terrible thing indeed, 7:1; Psalm 7:11.

Achan also brought trouble on Israel. The soldiers had to run away from their enemies and thirty-six of them were killed, 7:5. Achan himself had to die because of his sin, and he did not die alone. Perhaps you wonder why Achan's family had to die too. They had probably shared in his sin by helping him to carry or bury what he had stolen. We know that God, the Judge of the whole earth, will do what is just and right, Genesis 18:25.

Achan should have been a good example to his family, but instead it seems that he led them into sin. We should remember that each one of us has an effect on others, Romans 14:7. We are either leading people closer to God or we are showing them the wrong way. God is just and He returns trouble on those who trouble His people, 2 Thessalonians 1:6, but He also always remembers any good thing we do for a child of God.

In this chapter Achan's sons and daughters were put to death, but we do not know what their names were. The names of Achan's ancestors are given and they all share in his shame.

Achan could have had the things he wanted without stealing from God if he had waited just a little longer. God permitted the people of Israel to keep whatever they found in Ai, 8:2. We too should not go after the things of this world at the present time because later on we will rule with Christ in glory, 1 Corinthians 4.8; Revelation 20:6.

THE PEOPLE OF ISRAEL WON THE VICTORY AT AI,
chapter 8

1/19   The people of Israel were now ready to go ahead and win another victory. God had commanded Joshua to remove the wicked person from among them, 7:10-15; 1 Corinthians 5:13, and Joshua and the people had obeyed. God now promised to give them the victory and told them what they should do next. He told Joshua not to be discouraged but to go to Ai with the soldiers and have some of the men hide behind the city, 8:1,2.

1/20   Joshua chose 30,000 men, ten times as many as went to Ai the first time, 7:4. He then told the soldiers the plan and they went out secretly and hid themselves on the west side of Ai. The next day Joshua led all the other soldiers except 5,000 to the north side of the city. He sent the 5,000 men to help the 30,000 who were hidden on the west side, 8:12.

The following day the king of Ai came out to fight with Israel. Joshua and his men ran away from them as they had done before, 7:4, and all the men of Ai and Bethel went out after them and pursued them, 8:17.

1/21   Then the Lord commanded Joshua to stretch out his spear toward the city, as Moses had done with his rod, Exodus 7:19; 8:5; 9:23; 10:12,13; 14:16. Joshua did this and the men who were hiding behind the city ran into the city and set it on fire. The men of Ai looked behind them, saw the smoke and knew that Israel had taken their city. At the same time Joshua and his men turned around and killed all the men of Ai except the king, 8:23.

1/22   The men of Israel pursued the people of Ai and killed them all, 12,000 men and women. Joshua did not draw back his hand until they had won a complete victory. The men of Israel took the cattle and whatever else they wanted and then burned the city with fire, 8:27,28. The king of Ai had not been killed during the battle but Joshua hanged him on a tree until evening, Deuteronomy 21:23. After that they threw his body at the gate of the city and put a large pile of stones on top of it,

8:29. This pile of stones would help the people of Israel remember that the king of Ai was under a curse.

1/23   From Ai the people of Israel journeyed about 30 miles (50 kilometers) to Mount Ebal and Mount Gerizim. Moses had commanded Israel before his death to set up large stones on Mount Ebal and Mount Gerizim when they entered the land of Canaan, and to write on them the words of the Law. He also told them to build an altar of whole stones after they had set up the large stones, Deuteronomy 27:2-6.

God wanted His people to build the altar with stones which had not been shaped in any way with a tool of iron. The altar speaks to us of Christ dying for our sins. The work of the Lord Jesus Christ on the cross was perfect and none of our works can in any way add to it or help us to be saved, Exodus 20:25.

Joshua obeyed these commands of Moses, but he built the altar first. After that he wrote on the stones a copy of the Law and read it to the people, 8:32,34. Galatians 3:11 shows that no one can be saved by keeping the Law. First we need to be saved through the work which Christ has done for us on the cross and then the Holy Spirit can help us keep the Law, Romans 8:4.

Moses had also commanded that six tribes should stand before Mount Gerizim and the other six before Mount Ebal, Deuteronomy 27:11-13. Joshua gathered all the people, including the women and children, and the strangers who lived with the Israelites. He then read the blessings and curses of the Law which are found in Deuteronomy 28 before them all. This was a very strong warning to the people of Israel that they must obey the Law of Jehovah. They would have great blessing if they obeyed, but all God's judgments would come on them if they disobeyed.

We should obey the Lord because we love Him, but if we disobey Him He will bring trouble into our lives in order to bring us back to Himself.

TEST YOURSELF (Joshua 5-8)

1. Why did Joshua circumcise the men of Israel before he led them against their enemies?

2. What does the Passover speak of?

3. Who was the Captain of the armies of Israel?

4. What was saved when Israel burned Jericho? Write down three answers.

5. What happened later to Rahab?

6. Why were the men of Israel afraid at Ai?

7. Did Achan confess what he had done?

8. Who died because of Achan's sin?

9. How many soldiers went with Joshua the second time to take Ai?

10. What did Joshua do on Mount Ebal?

Turn to page 112 to check your answers.

3 TAKING POSSESSION OF THE LAND OF PROMISE

THE GIBEONITES, chapter 9

1/24   In the first eight chapters of this book we have seen Joshua and Israel entering the land of promise and getting the victory over Jericho. They were also able to destroy the city of Ai after they had punished the one who had sinned among them. In chapters 9-11 we see that Joshua and Israel fought with their enemies on the north and on the south and were able to defeat them.

The kings of six nations between Jordan and the Great Sea (the Mediterranean) heard of the victories Israel had won and they joined together to fight against them, 9:1,2. Lebanon is a mountain in the northern part of Palestine. The Jebusites lived in Jerusalem which is in the center of the land.

The men of Gibeon also heard what Joshua and Israel had done to Jericho and Ai. They did not want to fight with Israel and decided to try another plan to save themselves and their families. They put on old clothes and shoes and took old bottles and old bread and went to the Israelites in Gilgal. Men of three other cities came with them, 9:17. Gibeon was a large city west of Jericho and only about 15 miles (24 kilometers) from Gilgal, but the men acted as if they had made a very long journey. They asked the men of Israel to make an agreement with them and to promise not to fight against them, 9:6. However, the Lord had commanded Israel not to make peace with the nations of the land,
1/25   Deuteronomy 7:2. The men of Israel were afraid that perhaps these people really lived in the land, 9:7. So the Gibeonites turned to Joshua and lied again, saying that they had come from a far country, 9.8,9. They said that they had started their journey with fresh bread and new clothes and shoes and bottles, but now all were old.

It is always best to ask the Lord what to do when you are not quite sure yourself, but the Israelites did not do so. They believed the lie of the Gibeonites and made an agreement with them and swore not to kill them, 9:15.

1/26   Only three days later Israel found out that the Gibeonites really lived in the land of Canaan. They started at once to journey to their cities and reached them on the third day, 9:17. The people of Israel complained about the agreement their leaders had made, but the leaders had sworn by Jehovah that they would not fight against the Gibeonites **1/27**   and they could not break their promise. Instead they suggested that the men of Gibeon should serve the people of Israel by cutting the wood for their fires and by carrying their water from the river. Joshua called the Gibeonites and told them that they were under a curse because they had deceived the people of Israel. They would be slaves and would cut wood and carry water for the house of God. The men of Gibeon agreed to do this, 9.22-27.

Perhaps the people of Israel were glad to have other people do the hard work for them, but this chapter really shows that Israel failed. The Gibeonites were wicked people and would teach their evil ways to the young people of Israel. We shall see later that people of other nations were also allowed to live among the Israelites.

Rahab was different from the Gibeonites. She too told a lie, but the Gibeonites lied because they were afraid; Rahab had faith.

This chapter also shows us how Satan works. Sometimes he uses force against God's people and sometimes he tries to deceive them. The kings of Canaan got together and wanted to kill as many men of Israel as they could. The people of Israel could not defeat their enemies when someone among them disobeyed the Lord's commands or when they believed a lie. Often a lie sounds like the truth so we must ask the Lord to guide us at all times.

WAR IN THE SOUTH OF THE LAND, chapter 10

1/28   The Amorites were one of the six nations who lived in the south part of the land, 9:1. They had five kings, each one ruling over his own city. One of these was Adoni-Zedek, king of Jerusalem. This king felt that the Gibeonites had become enemies because they had made peace with Israel. So Adoni-Zedek sent messengers to the kings of Hebron, Jarmuth, Lachish, and Eglon and suggested that they go together to destroy Gibeon, 10:3,4.

The men of Gibeon had just escaped death by becoming the slaves of Israel, but now it looked as if they would be killed by the Amorites. The Gibeonites called Joshua to help them and Joshua and all the soldiers of Israel went to Gibeon, 10:7.

> Joshua went immediately to help the Gibeonites when they needed help. In the same way we can depend on the Lord Jesus Christ to help and look after His servants. He has bought us with His own blood and we are of great value to Him. He knows each one of us; He gives us eternal life and has promised that we will never die, John 10:27,28.

1/29   The Lord promised Joshua that He would give Israel the victory, 10.8. The men of Israel walked all night and suddenly came on the Amorites at Gibeon. No doubt the army was very tired when they arrived at Gibeon but the Lord helped them to defeat their enemies. First He made the Amorites very much afraid when the Israelites suddenly appeared and they tried to run away, but the Lord threw great hailstones from heaven which killed more Amorites than the swords of the Israelites did, 10:10,11.

Joshua was afraid that many of the Amorites would get away when it got dark at sunset, so in front of all the people he asked the Lord to keep the sun from going down. The Lord rewarded Joshua's faith and that day was almost as long as two days. The moon had already started to rise and it also seemed to stand still.

> Some people do not believe that miracles are possible, but God created the sun and the moon and the earth and He could certainly keep the earth from turning if He wanted to. Perhaps you wonder why He would want to do so. He did it to answer the prayer of His faithful servant Joshua who was trying to obey His commands.

1/30   So Joshua succeeded in saving the Gibeonites from their enemies and the people of Israel returned to their camp at Gilgal, 10:15.

Soon after that they heard that the five kings of the Amorites had hidden themselves in a cave at Makkedah. Joshua realized that this gave Israel an opportunity to defeat all the cities of the south. He commanded his men to guard the five kings and to pursue the rest of the Amorites. They caught many of them, but some were able to get into the big cities, 10:20.

2/1 Then Joshua brought the five kings out of the cave and the commanders of the army of Israel put their feet on their necks and killed them, 10:24,26. This was a sign that the Amorites had been completely defeated and it helped the Israelites to believe that the Lord would destroy all their enemies, 10:25.

2/2 After that Joshua and Israel took seven great cities: Makkedah, 10:28; Libnah, 10:29,30; Lachish, 10:31,32; Gezer, 10:33; Eglon, 10:34,35; Hebron, 10:36,37; and Debir, 10:38,39. Three of these cities, Hebron, Lachish, and Eglon had joined with Adoni-Zedek, king of Jerusalem, to fight against Gibeon, 10:3. So Joshua and Israel gained the victory over the whole southern part of the country, 10:40-43.

In Genesis 14:18 we read of Melchizedek, the friend of Abraham, and king of Salem. Salem was the old name for Jerusalem and Melchizedek means *king of righteousness*. Adoni-Zedek means *lord of righteousness*. He too was king of Jerusalem, but he was an enemy of the people of God. He was killed, but Israel did not take Jerusalem until the time of David, 2 Samuel 5:6,7.

WAR IN THE NORTH OF THE LAND, chapter 11

2/3 Now the nations in the north of the land joined together to fight against Israel. Hazor was a city north of the Sea of Galilee, the most important city of that part of the country. Jabin, king of Hazor, sent messengers to the other kings, and a great number of soldiers, too many to count, came together near the waters of Merom.

2/4 Joshua had been waiting for this opportunity and the Lord told him that He would give Israel victory the next day. The men of Israel believed this promise and bravely attacked their enemies, just as they had done before, 11:7; 10:9. Some of the enemy soldiers tried to run away, but the men of Israel followed them and killed them all. They cut the horses behind the knees and burned the war chariots as the Lord had commanded them to do, 11:6,9. The people of Israel might have put their trust in the horses and chariots instead of in the Lord if they had kept them.

Then Joshua went back to Hazor and destroyed it together with its king. He killed all the kings but did not burn the old cities except Hazor, 11:13. The Israelites killed all the men in the cities and took for themselves the cattle and anything else they wanted, 11:14.

2/5   In the last part of the chapter, verses 15 to 23, we read again a short account of the victories the Lord gave Israel. Israel took all the land from the south, 11:16, to the north, 11:17. It took them a long time, 11:18, and the Lord hardened the hearts of the people of the land so that they tried to fight against Israel. Only the people of Gibeon received mercy because they did not fight against them, 11:19.

Joshua even destroyed the Anakim who were very tall people, 11:21,22. Many years before this the men of Israel refused to enter the land of Canaan because they were afraid of the Anakim, Numbers 13:32,33. Apparently the men of Israel were not able to destroy them all at this time because some were left in Gaza, Gath, and Ashdod. One of these tall men of Gath caused Israel a lot of trouble later on, 1 Samuel 17:4.

LIST OF THE KINGS OF CANAAN, chapter 12

2/6   God did not allow Moses to cross the Jordan River and enter the land of promise, but Moses did lead Israel in defeating the great kings on the east side of Jordan, Sihon and Og, 12:1-6. The tribes of Reuben and Gad, and half the tribe of Manasseh, lived in this part of the land.

2/7   West of the Jordan Joshua and the men of Israel destroyed thirty-one kings, 12:7-24. The cities of these kings reached from Seir in the south to Lebanon in the north, 12:7. The names of these cities are given in verses 9 to 24. We do not know where they all were but Joshua gave this land to the people of Israel.

These events teach us that God helps those who believe in Him. No enemy can stand before the Christian who really trusts in the Lord. He will give you victory over sin in your own life if you obey Him even when you think you are too weak to do what He commands you to do. For example, the people of Israel had no horses or chariots but they defeated their enemies who were much better equipped than they, 11.6; Psalm 20.7.

The Lord gave Israel many victories, but we shall see that they also often failed and disobeyed the Lord. We have seen in these chapters that they left the men of Gibeon alive as well as some of the Anakim when they should have destroyed them the same as all the other people of the land, chapter 9; 11.22.

TEST YOURSELF (Joshua 9-12)

1. Why did the Gibeonites tell Joshua a lie?

2. Why did Joshua believe this lie?

3. How did the chief men punish the Gibeonites without breaking their promise to them?

4. What do we learn in chapter 9 about Satan's methods of attacking God's people?

5. Why did Joshua protect the people of Gibeon from the Amorites?

6. Name three ways in which the Lord helped Israel defeat the Amorites.

7. Could God really make the sun stand still?

8. Why did Joshua tell the chiefs of Israel to put their feet on the necks of five kings?

9. Show the difference between Melchizedek and Adoni-Zedek, kings of Jerusalem.

10. What happened to the kings of the north?

Turn to page 113 to check your answers.

4 THE DIVISION OF THE LAND

THE 2 ½ TRIBES, 13:1 - 14:5

2/8   The first twelve chapters of the book of Joshua tell about the great victories the Lord gave to Joshua and Israel. Now, in chapter 13, we read that Joshua was getting old and Israel still did not possess all the land, 13:1. The Philistines still occupied large portions of the land even though the men of one of their cities, Eglon, had been destroyed, 10:34,35. Also around Lebanon in the north there were people whom Israel had not yet driven out. The time had come, however, to divide the whole land among the nine and a half tribes and the Lord promised to drive out the rest of their enemies, 13.6,7.

2/9   Moses had already described the borders on the east of the river Jordan, Deuteronomy 3.8-17, but now this land is described more carefully, and we see again that Israel did not drive out all their enemies, 13.8-13.

2/10   Moses did not give any part of the land to the tribe of Levi, 13:14,33. The Levites served the Lord and could not raise their own food. The other tribes were to bring their offerings to Jehovah, and part of these offerings were for the Levites, Numbers 18:20-24.

The tribe of Reuben received a large piece of land east of the northern half of the Dead Sea. The borders of this land are described in verses 15-23.

2/11   We read again that Balaam died with the enemies of the Lord's people, 13:22; Numbers 31.8. Balaam was a false prophet, but God spoke to him and through him. Balaam greatly desired to have the money that Balak, the king of Moab, offered him, but God would not allow Balaam to curse Israel, so Balak found another way to bring God's judgment on His people, Numbers 25:1; Revelation 2:14. Balaam wanted and got the money of the Moabites but he was also killed together with them by the Israelites.

Today some Christians want to join with unbelievers in their pleasures and sins. They may have to suffer with them also.

The land of the tribe of Gad was north of the land of Reuben and also east of Jordan. Their land extended to the river Jabbok and a little north of it. They even had a narrow piece of land on the banks of Jordan as far north as the Sea of Galilee which is here called the Sea of Chinnereth, 13:27.

2/12   The half tribe of Manasseh received the rest of the country east of Jordan including sixty cities, 13:29-31. We must remember that God did not intend that some of the tribes should live east of Jordan. It would have been much better if all the people had lived in the land which the Lord had chosen for them. Israel never did drive out all their enemies on the west of Jordan. We cannot be wiser than God but should obey His commands even when we do not understand the reason for them.

2/13   Joshua and Eleazar the priest gave a part of the land to each of the 9½ tribes. These two men did not decide by themselves which part of the land each tribe should have but God revealed to them His will in this matter by drawing lots, 14:1,2; Proverbs 16:33. In this way no tribe could complain that another tribe was getting a better part of the land.

It is wonderful to know that God is caring for us. Let us never grumble because someone else is enjoying greater blessings than we are.

We read again that Levi did not get any part of the land, 14:3, but the men of Joseph were counted as two tribes, Manasseh and Ephraim, Genesis 48:5, so there were still twelve tribes to occupy the land, 14:4,5.

CALEB, 14.6-15

2/14   Caleb was the son of a Kenizzite who lived among the people of Judah. Moses had sent him and Joshua and ten other men to see what the land of Canaan was like, Numbers 13.6. When they came back only Caleb and Joshua told the people that God would give Israel the victory.

Here Caleb called Moses the man of God and the servant of God, 14:6,7. Moses had promised forty-five years before this that Caleb would have the land which he had walked on for his inheritance. All the men of Israel who had left Egypt had died in the desert except Joshua and Caleb, and now Caleb was eighty-five years old. He was as strong as ever, 14:10,11, so he asked Joshua to give him the hill country where the tall Anakim lived in strong cities, 14:12.

It is good to see that Caleb was still brave and still a man of faith even at this time of his life. Some Christians feel it is all right for them to take things easier when they get older and their faith is not as strong as before.

Caleb's faith was as strong when he was eighty-five as it had been when he was young, and he was still willing to fight the battles of the Lord. Joshua was happy to see this and he gave Caleb the land he asked for, 14:13-15.

Caleb said that he had followed the Lord with his whole heart, and carried out God's purposes, 14:8. Moses and the writer of this book said the same thing about him, 14:9,14. This is what God wants you and me to do, to love Him with our whole heart and soul and mind, Matthew 22:37. Let us not be Christians who follow the Lord on Sunday but live for ourselves and the things of the world the other six days of the week!

JUDAH, chapter 15

2/15   After this we have a long list of places on the borders of the land given to Judah, 15:1-12. You will be able to find some of these places on a good map. Note that the city of Jerusalem was given to Judah but they never really took this city until the time of David, 2 Samuel 5:6,7. The Lord also gave Judah a piece of land which stretched to the Mediterranean Sea, 15:12, but even in the time of David the Philistines were still living there and kept attacking the people of Israel.

2/16   Caleb, however, took full possession of the land which he had been given. He took the city of Hebron and drove out the Anakim who lived there, 15:13,14. Then Caleb called for some young man to take the city of Debir. Othniel, his brother's son, took this city and Caleb gave him his daughter Achsah to be his wife. He also gave them a piece of land and springs of water, 15:18,19.

2/17   God had told His people not to marry someone from their own family, Leviticus 18:6-18, but Othniel married the daughter of his father's brother. However, Othniel showed that he had faith and courage when he took the city of Debir and later he became one of the judges of Israel, Judges 3:9.

2/18   The remaining part of the chapter is a long list of cities and villages belonging to Judah, 112 cities and eleven villages. Among them were three Philistine cities, Ekron, Ashdod, and Gaza, 15:45-47. The people of Judah gave up fighting their enemies before they had completely defeated them and allowed the Jebusites of Jerusalem to live among them, 15:63.

> We must follow the Lord *with our whole heart* if we want to get the full victory over all our enemies. The important lesson of the books of Joshua and Judges is this: The Lord gave Israel the whole land, but they did not take possession of it all. They could have defeated all their enemies, but they gave up too soon.

EPHRAIM AND MANASSEH, chapters 16,17

2/19   Chapters 16 and 17 tell about the land which was given to the tribes of Joseph, Ephraim and Manasseh. The Lord gave a large part of the land to the tribe of Ephraim, 16:5-9, but the men of Ephraim did not drive out the Canaanites who lived in Gezer, 16:10. They allowed them to live but forced them to work for them without receiving any pay. This means that they disobeyed God's command to destroy all the people of the land. Later these Canaanites led Israel to sin against God by worshiping their idols.

2/20   Seven families of the tribe of Manasseh received part of the land on the east side of the Jordan River, 17:1,2. The five daughters of Zelophehad also received an inheritance with their male relatives, 17:3-6, as Moses had commanded, Numbers 27:6,7.

2/21   The other half of the tribe of Manasseh received land on the west side of Jordan, but were not able to drive out the Canaanites, 17:7-13.

2/22   The Lord had told Joshua and Eleazar to give a large portion of land to the tribes of Ephraim and Manasseh, but the men of these two tribes were not able to drive out all the Canaanites who lived in that land, 16:10; 17:13. They came to Joshua to ask him for more land and said that there was not enough room for them all, 17:14. Joshua told them they would have sufficient room if they drove out the Perizzites, but the men of Ephraim and Manasseh said that these Canaanites were too strong for them, 17:15,16. Joshua answered them wisely saying that they would be able to drive out the Canaanites if they had faith and courage.

Today also there are many people who want victory without fighting for it. Others do very little work and a lot of complaining about others. We should work together for the Lord and not grumble.

THE OTHER TRIBES, chapters 18,19

2/23   Shiloh was the capital city of Israel until the time of King David. The Ark was kept there until David brought it to Jerusalem, 2 Samuel 6:12.

God had given Israel victory throughout the whole country, but seven tribes still did not have any land. Joshua sent three men from each tribe to divide the remaining land into seven parts. Judah, Ephraim, and Manasseh already had land, Levi did not get any, and Reuben and Gad had land east of Jordan. Joshua told these twenty-one men to write down in a book the names of the towns, rivers, and mountains. Then he drew lots for each tribe, 18:2-10.

2/24   Verses 11-28 give the names of the towns and borders of the land given to Benjamin. It was north and east of Judah but south of Ephraim and included Jebus or Jerusalem, but neither Judah nor Benjamin were able to drive out the Jebusites who lived there, 15:63; Judges 1:21.

2/25   The tribe of Simeon received the southern part of the land that had been given to Judah because Judah had more than they needed, 19:1-9. This land included the cities of Sheba, Moladah, Beersheba, Hormah, Ziklag, and Ain, 15:26-32.

2/26   Zebulun received land with twelve cities north of that of Manasseh, 19:10-16.

2/27   Issachar's land was north of that of Manasseh and between the land of Zebulun and the river Jordan. Issachar received sixteen cities, 19:17-23.

2/28   Asher received land which was north of Zebulun, reached to the Mediterranean Sea and included twenty-two cities, 19:24-31.

2/29   Naphtali was west of Asher and north of Zebulun and Issachar, 19:32-39. Their land reached to the Jordan and had nineteen cities in it.

2/30   The seventh and last tribe was Dan and they received land between Judah and Ephraim, west of Benjamin, 19:40-48. Some of their cities were near the Mediterranean Sea but the Danites were not able to drive out the Philistines. Later some of the men of Dan went to the country north of Naphtali, took the city of Leshem or Laish, and changed the name of the city to Dan, 19:47; Judges 18:7, 27-29.

3/1   Finally Israel gave Joshua the city of Timnath-serah in the land of Ephraim as the Lord had commanded. Joshua had wanted this city and so he was very pleased, 19:49,50. People always live together happily when they know and do the will of God.

THE CITIES OF REFUGE, chapter 20

3/2   Now God told Joshua to choose six *cities of refuge*. He had commanded Israel to put to death anyone who killed someone else. However, someone might kill another person accidentally. In this case the guilty person could run to a place where he would be safe, Exodus 21:12-14. The Lord had told Moses to set aside six cities for this purpose, Numbers 35:9-34, and later Moses told Israel again to do this, Deuteronomy 19:2-13. Now the Lord told Joshua and Israel to set aside these six cities, 20.1-6. Anyone who killed a person by accident could run to one of these cities of refuge to save himself from the relatives of the dead man who would try to take vengeance. The killer had to stay inside the city of refuge until his case was examined by the judge or until the high priest died. After that he was free to return to his family.

> The city of refuge is a picture of the Lord Jesus Christ. We are guilty sinners but we can run to the Savior and be safe from God's judgment.

3/3   The people of Israel obeyed this command of the Lord and chose Kadesh in the north, Shechem in the center, and Hebron in the south. They also chose Bezer, Ramoth, and Golan as cities of refuge on the east side of Jordan. In this way no Israelite would have to go very far in order to get to a city of refuge.

> The Lord set aside these six cities, but we do not read about anyone who ran to one of them to save himself from those who wanted to take vengeance. Some did run to the altar in the tabernacle or the temple for safety, 1 Kings 2:28. Today many people do not know God's way of salvation, or do not accept it for themselves, just as we do not read of people using the cities of refuge. These people are lost and God's wrath rests on them, John 3:36. For this reason God has commanded us to tell all men about His love and the wonderful salvation which He has provided for them.

THE CITIES OF THE LEVITES, chapter 21

3/4   All the tribes had now received land except the Levites. God had promised that they should have cities, but not land, 14:4; Numbers 35:1-8. However, with each city there was to be enough land for their cattle. The chief Levites now approached Joshua and Eleazar the priest and the elders of the tribes about this matter, 21:1-3.

3/5   Levi had three sons, Kohath, Gershon, and Merari. Aaron belonged to the family of Kohath. The sons of Aaron received 13 cities, the other sons of Kohath 10, the sons of Gershon 13, and of Merari 12; 48 cities in all, 21:4-8.

3/6   Simeon had part of the land of Judah, 19:1, and these two tribes gave nine cities to the sons of Aaron, including Hebron, a city of refuge. Hebron belonged to Caleb, 15:13, and he kept the land and the villages around the city, 21:12. Caleb also gave Debir to the family of Aaron, 15:15; 21:15.

Benjamin also gave four cities to the family of Aaron, 21:17,18.

3/7   The rest of the family of Kohath received Shechem, a city of refuge, and three others from Ephraim, four from Dan, and two from the half tribe of Manasseh on the west of Jordan, ten in all, 21:20-26.

3/8   The family of Gershon received Golan, a city of refuge, and one more from the half tribe of Manasseh on the east side of Jordan. Issachar and Asher gave them four cities each, and Naphtali gave to Gershon Kedesh, another city of refuge, and two others. This makes 13 cities for the family of Gershon, 21:27-33.

3/9   Last of all Zebulun gave the family of Merari four cities west of Jordan. Reuben gave them Bezer and three others east of Jordan, and Gad gave them Ramoth and three others, also east of Jordan. Bezer and Ramoth were both cities of refuge, 20:8. So Merari received twelve cities altogether. All the Levites together had 42 cities as well as the six cities of refuge and land for their animals, 21:34-42.

3/10   These things show us that God did everything He had promised to do. The Levites had special work to do for the Lord and did not get any land of their own but God gave them cities to live in and commanded the people of Israel to give them one tenth of all they received themselves, Numbers 18:21.

God wanted the priests and Levites to teach His Law to the people, Leviticus 10:11; 2 Chronicles 35:3; Nehemiah 8:9. There were cities of the Levites in each of the twelve tribes of Israel. Each tribe gave them four cities, except Judah and Simeon who gave nine, and Naphtali in the far north gave only three. So we see that God prepares for the spiritual needs of His people and for the material needs of His servants who teach them.

The chapter ends with another statement that God had fulfilled all His promises, 21:45; 11:23. He always does and always will.

TEST YOURSELF (Joshua 13-21)

1. Which tribes settled east of Jordan?

2. Why did Israel kill Balaam?

3. What did Caleb ask for when he was 85 years old?

4. Why did Caleb let his daughter marry Othniel?

5. Which tribe was given the city of Jerusalem?

6. Why did Ephraim and Manasseh complain to Joshua?

7. Why did the tribes come to Shiloh?

8. What city did Joshua himself receive?

9. What were the cities of refuge?

10. What land did the Levites get?

Turn to page 114 to check your answers.

5 THE LAST WORDS OF JOSHUA

THE 2 ½ TRIBES RETURNED HOME, chapter 22

3/11   God allowed the 2½ tribes to have land east of Jordan but it was not really His will for them to live there.

Sometimes we demand things from God that we want very much and God gives them to us even though they are not really His will for us, Psalm 106:15. We should always pray as the Lord Jesus did, *Not my will, but Your will be done,* Luke 22:42.

The 2½ tribes had promised to help the other tribes defeat the nations west of Jordan, and take their land, 1:16. Forty thousand of them had fulfilled their promise and had crossed the Jordan to fight with the other Israelites, 4:13, and now Joshua praised them because they had obeyed his commands, 22:1-3. He told them that they could go back home but he commanded them to continue to love the Lord and to obey His Law. Then he blessed them. God blesses His people only when they obey Him.

3/12   The men of Reuben, Gad, and Manasseh had also received much cattle, gold, silver, and other things from their battles. Joshua told them to share these riches with the people of their tribes who had stayed at home, 22:7-9.

Some years later David told his men to do the same, 1 Samuel 30:24. Our Lord has commanded us to preach the Gospel to every creature. Some people are not able to leave home but they can help those who do go. They too will share in the reward which the Lord will give to His faithful servants when He comes back again.

So the 2½ tribes started their journey home. They came to the Jordan River and built a great altar before they crossed the river. The people of the other tribes became very angry when they heard about this and **3/13** went to stop them, 22:10-12. They first sent Phinehas the priest together with the ten leading men of Israel to ask the soldiers of Reuben, Gad, and Manasseh about the altar, 22:13,14. They accused the 2½ tribes of rebelling against God by building another altar. They were afraid that God would punish the whole nation as He had done at Baal-peor, Numbers 25:3. The leaders of Israel told the 2½ tribes they could live on the west side of the Jordan with the other tribes if they wanted to, 22:19. God had been angry with the whole nation of Israel when Achan sinned, 22:20; 7:1; now the 2½ tribes were making Him angry again.

3/14   The 2½ tribes did not agree with what the leaders of Israel had said, 22:21-29. They said the Lord knew that they had not built this altar in order to rebel against Him. The altar at Shiloh was for offering sacrifices to Jehovah, Joshua 18:1, but the purpose of this new altar was to help the ten tribes west of the Jordan remember that the people on the east side of the river also belonged to Israel. It was to be a witness to the people of Israel in the future.

3/15   Phinehas and the ten leaders were greatly relieved when they heard this answer. They were sure now that God was with Israel and would not be angry with them, 22:30,31. They brought this message back to the people and they too were very pleased. The 2½ tribes called their altar *Witness*.

What can we learn from this chapter?

1. We should not judge others before we know why they are acting as they do. Israel was ready to fight against their brothers before they knew what the 2½ tribes had in mind.

2. On the other hand the 2½ tribes should have talked with their brothers before doing anything which others might not understand. There has been a lot of trouble in many churches because some Christians have started to do things without telling the others about it. There is even greater trouble when we judge one another without asking *why* the other person acted the way he did.

3. Christians often do things which God has not commanded them to do. We have seen that the 2½ tribes chose to live east of

Jordan. God allowed them to do so but He knew it would have been better for all the twelve tribes to live together. We do not read that God told the 2½ tribes to build this altar, or that they even asked God about it. God's plan was to bring all the tribes together three times a year in order to remind them that they were all one, Deuteronomy 16:16. Trouble always results when we try to do things in our own wisdom.

David thought it would be a good idea to build a house for God, but he was willing to wait when he learned that it was not God's will for this house to be built at that time, 2 Samuel 7:1-7. Paul wanted to preach in the cities of Asia but the Holy Spirit led him on to do more important work, Acts 16:6-9. Let us do *everything* the Bible commands us *the way* God wants us to do it and *at the time* He wants it done, without following human wisdom.

THE LAST MESSAGE OF JOSHUA, chapters 23,24

3/16   Many years passed and finally the Israelites did not need to fight any longer. Joshua was over 100 years old and his work was finished. He knew that he would not live much longer, so he called the leaders of Israel together to give them a final message.

Joshua reminded the leaders how the Lord had helped Israel, 23:3-5. He told them that God would continue to help them, but Israel should obey God's laws and commands and must not have any fellowship with the nations around them, 23:6-11. He would not continue to give them victory if they mixed with the nations of the land, 23:12,13.

3/17   Then Joshua said that God had fulfilled all the promises He had given Israel, 23:14. In the same way He would fulfill all His warnings, and He would be angry with Israel if they disobeyed His commandments, 23:15,16.

It is the same today. God has told us not to have fellowship with unbelievers, 2 Corinthians 6:14-18. He wants all our love for Himself, 1 John 2:15, and it is impossible for us to love God and the world at the same time.

3/18   Then Joshua called the people to Shechem and spoke to them there, chapter 24. He told them about all the blessings God had

given them. Abraham's father had worshiped idols but God had called Abraham and blessed him. In verses 3-13 we read about sixteen things which Jehovah had done from the time of Abraham to the time of
3/19   Joshua. He had delivered Israel from Egypt, 24:5-7; from the Amorites, the Moabites, and many other nations, 24.8-12, and had given them a good land, 24:13. Therefore Israel should be determined to serve Jehovah. If they refused to serve the Lord they might be drawn into worshiping the gods of Abraham's ancestors or the gods of the people of the land, but Joshua had decided that he and his family would serve the Lord, 24:14,15.

3/20   Most people follow a leader and the people decided to follow Joshua's example and to serve the Lord, 24:16-18. Joshua warned them that God was holy and would not forgive them if they rebelled against Him. The people repeated that they would serve the Lord and agreed to put away their false gods, 24:19-24. Then Joshua
3/21   made a covenant with them in the name of the Lord, wrote it in a book and added it to the Law of Moses, Genesis to Deuteronomy. He then set up a great stone under a tree in Shechem which would be a witness to Israel in years to come of what they had promised to do, 24:25-28.

The people of Israel lived in tents while they traveled through the desert, 3:14, but now they were settled in the land of Canaan, so every man returned to the piece of land he had been given as his inheritance, 24:28.

Some day our journey through this world will be over too and we will have won our last victory. We will then live forever in heaven with our wonderful Savior.

Joshua did everything he could to help the people remember what the Lord had done for them. God has done much more for us. He gave His Son to die on the cross for us. He has given us the whole Bible, and the Holy Spirit lives in us. God has blessed us with every spiritual gift, Ephesians 1:3, and He wants to give us victory every day, 2 Corinthians 2:14. He has asked us to remember Him by breaking bread, 1 Corinthians 11:23-26.

3/22   The last part of the chapter tells us about Joshua's death. Joshua died when he was 110 years old, so he lived almost as long as

Moses, Deuteronomy 34.7. At this time the people buried the bones of Joseph, 24:32; Genesis 50:25; Exodus 13:19. Eleazar died also and was buried.

The people of Israel followed Jehovah while Joshua lived and the other elders who lived longer than he. The book of Judges tells us what happened after that.

Both Joshua and Eleazar were pictures of the Lord Jesus Christ. The name Joshua means Savior and is the same as Jesus in the New Testament. Eleazar is a picture of the Lord Jesus Christ, our Great High Priest, Hebrews 7:24-27. In this chapter we read about the death of both Joshua and Eleazar. Let us praise God that our Savior and High Priest will never die again. He has saved us from our sins; He prays for us and gives us victory over our sins every day. In the end He will take us to heaven to be with Him for ever.

The Teaching of Joshua

3/23   *Take a piece of paper about as big as this whole page and cover*
up everything on this page except what you are reading just
now. You can move the paper down a little at a time so you can read
more. Each paragraph or section of the page has a line under it. A para-
graph with a line under it is called a frame. You should read only one
frame at a time, and keep the rest of the page covered with the piece of
paper. Each frame will tell you a little more.

Each frame also has a question or a space at the end. This is to
see if you have understood the main teaching of the frame. Try to answer
the question or write the missing word in the empty space. If you cannot
answer the question, read the frame again. When you think you know the
right answer, move the paper down so you can see the next frame. Before
you read anything in the next frame, look first at the right side of the
frame. This gives the correct answer to the question in the first frame. If
you had the right answer, this shows that you have understood the most
important part of the first frame. You are now ready to go on to read
everything in the second frame. IF you did not get the right answer, you
are not ready to go on. You should read the first frame again and really
try to understand it. When you understand the first frame then you can
go on to the second frame. Read this frame carefully and answer the
question at the end. Then go on to the third frame and all the others, one
by one.

1   In the book of Joshua we often read that God spoke to Joshua and
seven times it says that God had spoken to Moses, 1:3; 11:15. The
people believed that God had spoken to Moses and they went to Joshua
to ask for something God had promised before, as for example Caleb
did, 14:9; and the daughters of Zelophehad, 17:3,4. This shows that they
believed the books of Moses are _____ .

----

1. the Word of God

2   What can we learn about God in the book of Joshua? God sent hail
from the sky to help His people and He also made the day of victory

48

much longer. God could do these great miracles; He must have _____ power.

— · — · — · — · — · — · — · — · — · — · — · — · — · — · — · —

2. all

3 God knew the sin of Achan, 7:1, and He knew the true reason of the men of Reuben and Gad for building an altar, 22:22. We can say that God knows _____ .

— · — · — · — · — · — · — · — · — · — · — · — · — · — · — · —

3. everything

4 The people had to make themselves clean, 3:5, and they had to circumcise all the men and boys before God would bless them, 5:3-5. Joshua knew that Jehovah is a _____ God, 24:19.

— · — · — · — · — · — · — · — · — · — · — · — · — · — · — · —

4. holy

5 God must also judge sin. He commanded Israel to destroy the wicked men in Canaan. Balaam had partly obeyed God's Word but he was killed with the enemies of the Lord. We can see that God is *righteous* and so He must _____ sinners.

— · — · — · — · — · — · — · — · — · — · — · — · — · — · — · —

3/24   *5. judge or punish*

6 God is the God of mercy. He judged the enemies of Israel but showed _____ to His own people.

— · — · — · — · — · — · — · — · — · — · — · — · — · — · — · —

6. mercy

7 God is always faithful. He promised to be with Joshua, 1:5, and He kept His promise to the very end, 21:45; 23:14. God always keeps His promises; God is_____ .

— · — · — · — · — · — · — · — · — · — · — · — · — · — · — · —

7. faithful

8 Can we learn anything about the Lord Jesus in the book of Joshua? The name Joshua means the same as Jesus. Joshua is in the old Jewish language while Jesus is the same as Joshua in the Greek language of the New Testament. You can see from Matthew 1:21 that Jesus means Savior. What does Joshua mean? _____ .

— · — · — · — · — · — · — · — · — · — · — · — · — · — · — · —

8. savior

9   Joshua saved Israel from their enemies, but the Lord Jesus saves us from_____.

—·—

9. sin

10 God gave victory to Israel through Joshua. How do we win victories today? 1 Corinthians 15:57; 2 Corinthians 2:14. _____
_____.

—·—

3/25   *10. Through our Lord Jesus Christ*

11 The Bible teaches that men have free will. They can choose what is right or what is wrong. Read Joshua 7:1 and 24:15 and name one man who chose the right and one who chose the wrong._____
_____.

—·—

11. Joshua; Achan

12 Joshua shows us a great deal about the sin of the Canaanites. God is righteous and had to punish them. But all men are sinners. How can God save anyone? Only because the Lord Jesus died for us as the Lamb of God. The people of Israel killed the Passover lamb, 5:10, and Joshua built an altar, 8:30, and sacrificed offerings on it. These offerings are pictures of our Lord Jesus Christ. How can God save a sinner?_____
_____.

—·—

12. A Sacrifice has died for us.

13 God forgives our sins through Christ, but He also gives us many other blessings. As believers we cannot enjoy these blessings until we learn that we are dead to sin and alive to God, Romans 6:11. We have a picture of this in Joshua because the people of Israel did not enjoy the blessings of Canaan until they crossed the Jordan River. The Jordan River speaks of death and we have been put to death with Christ on the cross, Galatians 2:19,20.

We can enjoy all God's blessings only when we see that we have been _____.

—·—

13. crucified with Christ

14 The cities of refuge make us think of the Lord Jesus Christ. The sinner can run to Christ and be _____ or find a Refuge.

---

14. safe

15 God blesses men only if they have faith. The book of Joshua has some wonderful examples of faith. Read Joshua 14:12 and Hebrews 11:31 and name two people of faith._____
_____.

3/26   *15. Caleb; Rahab*

16 God wants us to believe in Him and He tries to make our faith stronger. For example, the spies brought back news of Jericho which strengthened Joshua's faith, 2:24. The Lord Himself gave Joshua a special message to strengthen his faith, 11:6. If we believe in God He will make our _____ stronger.

---

16. faith

17 When Joshua showed faith, God did a great miracle for His people, 10:12,13. On the other hand, sometimes Israel went ahead in their own wisdom (for example, in the matter of the Gibeonites), and they had to suffer for it, 9:14,18. Today also God honors our faith but He will punish _____.

---

17. unbelief

18 If we have faith in God we should obey His commands. In the book of Joshua Jehovah commanded Joshua to obey the Law, 1:8. Through the whole book, we see Joshua obeying the Law and the Word of Jehovah. For example, Joshua did as the Lord commanded him at Jericho, 6:3,4,11,20. Joshua did as the Lord commanded him, 11:9, and he commanded the people to obey the Lord, 23:6, and to love Him, 22:5; 23:11. Joshua and the people obeyed the Law of Moses as the Law of Jehovah, 8:29-35; 10:26.

True faith results in_____.

---

18. obedience or good works, James 2:26

19   Faith also helps us win the victory in our daily struggle with sin, 1 John 5:4. Through faith Joshua won the victory at Jericho, chapter 6; at Ai, chapter 8; in the south country, 10:40-42; and in the north, 11:23.

What made the walls of Jericho fall down? Hebrews 11:30.

_____ .

19. faith

20   Were the people of Israel always victorious? 15:63; 17:10.

_____ .

3/27   *20. No, their faith sometimes failed*

21   God gave Israel the whole land but they only possessed the part of the land which they fought for and entered. This speaks to us of the many blessings which we have in Christ. God has given us many things but we must go forward in faith, fight against our enemies, and enter into the blessing. Some people do not like to work or fight. For example, Ephraim and Manasseh thought that Joshua should give them more land, 17:14, and he told them to fight for it. The other tribes also were slow in taking their land, 18:3.

God has given us many blessings, but we must _____ _____ before we get the victory.

21. believe, and fight and enter in

22   The Old Testament does not teach about the Church; this truth is revealed to us in the New Testament, Ephesians 3:4,5. However, there are pictures and lessons for the Church in the book of Joshua.

The people of Israel worshiped God when they kept the Passover, 5:10, which looked forward to the death of Christ. The Church should come together and break bread, which means to look back to the death of Christ. We can_____God when we break bread and remember the Lord and His death.

22. worship

23 How are believers like the tribe of Levi, 1 Peter 2:5? Some of the men of Levi were_____and all believers today are the same.

- -

23. priests

24 Some churches do things according to their own wisdom instead of following the Word of God. They should learn a lesson from the altar of Reuben, Gad, and Manasseh, 22:10. These tribes built a big altar and it caused trouble in Israel. They should have done God's will instead of acting according to man's_____.

- -

24. wisdom

25 Is the land of Canaan a picture of Heaven? Some people think so, but Israel had to fight against their enemies in Canaan. We believers have warfare and struggle now, Ephesians 6:12, but it will all be over when we get to Heaven.

Canaan was the land of victory and we can think of Canaan as a picture of the Christian today who_____the evil one, 1 John 2:14.

- -

25. masters

We can gain victory over Satan, James 4.7, and this brings glory to the Lord Jesus.

6 AFTER JOSHUA DIED

3/28   God had given the land of Canaan to Abraham and his children. The people of Canaan were very wicked and God did not want this evil to spread to other nations, so He commanded the people of Israel to destroy the Canaanites and to take their land. We saw in the book of Joshua that Joshua and Israel obeyed this command. We also saw that Israel won many victories and that they failed a few times. But in Judges we see Israel failing many times and winning only a few victories.

The book of Judges has three main parts. In chapters 1 and 2 we learn that the people continued to fight for the land after Joshua died, but they often failed. In chapters 3-16 we see that God often raised up a judge to lead the people of Israel. The people fell into sin again and again and each time their enemies defeated them. In their trouble Israel repented and turned back to the Lord. Then God chose a man to judge Israel and to lead them to victory against their enemies. These chapters tell us of fourteen judges who lived during this time.

The last five chapters tell about the terrible things that happened in Israel during these years when everyone did as he pleased, 21:25, but in the book of Ruth we see that even at that time there were some who followed the Lord.

ISRAEL FAILED TO DRIVE OUT THE NATIONS OF CANAAN, *chapter 1*

In chapter 1 Israel sometimes won the victory and sometimes failed. In verses 1-21 we read about Judah, Simeon, and Benjamin. The people first asked the Lord who should go to fight against the Canaanites. Joshua belonged to the tribe of Ephraim, but now God began to show that Judah would become the leading tribe. David and finally the Lord Jesus Himself were born of the tribe of Judah. Even today the people of Israel are called Jews, a word which comes from the name Judah.

God promised to give the land to the tribe of Judah, but the men of Judah felt they would not be able to take it alone, so they asked the men of Simeon to go with them, 1:2,3. They made Adoni-Bezek, king of Bezek, their prisoner, and cut off his thumbs and his great toes. Adoni-Bezek agreed that this was fair because he himself had done the same thing to seventy other kings, 1:7. God had commanded Israel to destroy the people of Canaan, but the men of Judah and Simeon allowed Adoni-Bezek to live for a while.

3/29   Then the men of Judah took Jerusalem and burned it, 1:8. They also took Hebron, 1:10.

In verses 11 to 15 we read again about Caleb and Othniel. Othniel showed that he had courage and faith when he took the town of Debir and Caleb allowed him to marry his daughter Achsah. Caleb also gave them wells of water when Achsah asked for them.

We already read about Othniel and Achsah in Joshua 15:14-19. God is always pleased when His people have faith, especially young people. This is the reason why the Holy Spirit told us twice about Othniel and Achsah.

3/30   In the next part of the chapter, verses 16 to 21, the Kenites and the tribe of Simeon helped the men of Judah. They took the city of Hormah and three large Philistine cities, Gaza, Askelon, and Ekron. The Lord was with the men of Judah, 1:19, but their faith was small and they were not able to drive out the people who lived in the valley. These Canaanites were very strong soldiers, but of course the Lord was stronger than they. Caleb was able to take Hebron, but the men of Benjamin were not able to drive out completely the Jebusites who lived in Jerusalem. Some of them continued to live there until the time the book of Judges was written, 1:21. Israel finally took complete possession of Jerusalem during the time of King David. In verse 19 we see the first sign that the people of Israel would fail and in the rest of the chapter we see them failing again and again.

4/1   The tribes of Joseph, Ephraim and Manasseh, succeeded at first, then failed, 1:22-29. They were able to take Bethel when they found a man who showed them the way to get into the city. They did not kill this man and his family together with all the other people of the city, but he did not believe in the Lord as Rahab had done, 1:25; Joshua 6:25. He built another city and called it by the name of the old one, 1:26,23. Manasseh did not drive out the inhabitants of five cities, 1:27. The Canaanites continued to live in the land but had to work for Israel at certain times, 1:28. They continued to live also in Gezer among the people of Ephraim, 1:29.

4/2   In the last part of the chapter we read about the failure of four other tribes. Zebulun did not drive out the men of two cities, 1:30, and Asher failed in seven cities, 1:31. Naphtali did not destroy the people of two cities, but lived with them, 1:33. The Amorites were stronger than the men of Dan and forced them to live in the hills, 1:34. However, later Dan became strong and made the Amorites work for them. God had commanded Israel to *destroy* the people of the land because they were evil, and it was a sin for Israel to let them live.

This chapter teaches us that sometimes God commands us to do difficult things and that He gives us power to do them. He will also help us to put away all sin from our lives if we are willing to do so. We will never be able to grow strong in the work of the Lord if we do not overcome our bad habits.

ISRAEL SINNED AFTER THE DEATH OF JOSHUA,

chapter 2

4/3   In the first chapter of Judges we saw Israel winning some victories as they had done in the book of Joshua, but they also failed many times. As time went on they failed more and more. Chapter 2 tells us that they failed because they forgot the Lord so often.

In the first part of this chapter the angel of the Lord spoke to the people. Perhaps this was a prophet speaking in the name of Jehovah because the word *angel* also means *messenger*. However, in Genesis 22 the One called the Angel of the Lord was really the Son of God who came from the Father to show God's will to men, Genesis 22:11, 12,15,16.

God reminded Israel of how He had blessed them and what He had commanded them to do. They had been slaves in Egypt but now God had given them their own land. He had commanded them not to make an agreement with the people of the land, but to destroy the altars of their false gods. Israel had not obeyed this command and now God said to them, *Look what you have done!*

God has the right to ask men to give an account of what they do. He talked in the same way to Eve, Genesis 3:13, and to Cain, Genesis 4:10. Christians must also give an account to God, Romans 14:12; 2 Corinthians 5:10; Matthew 25:19. Let us be careful of how we live so that we will be able to give this account with joy.

The Lord would no longer give Israel the victory because they had disobeyed Him, 2:3. The people were very sorry when they heard these words and they wept. For this reason they called the place Bochim which means *weeping*, and offered sacrifices to the Lord. In later years God often sent His prophets and messengers to bring the people of Israel back to Himself. Sometimes the people listened to the prophet and confessed their sins. At other times they killed the prophet or messenger and kept on sinning. At Bochim they repented of their sins but before long they started to sin again.

4/4   The Angel said these things to Israel while Joshua was still living and in verses 6 to 10 we read that Israel followed the Lord most of the time while Joshua was still alive and also during the time of the elders who lived longer than Joshua. However, the children and young people were not willing to follow Jehovah when they grew up but started to worship other gods, the Baals and Ashtaroth. This made the Lord angry and He allowed their enemies to defeat them when Israel tried to fight against them. The Lord had warned them before that this would happen if they disobeyed Him, 2:15; Deuteronomy 28:15,25. It happened very often in the times of the judges.

4/5   Israel cried to the Lord when they got into trouble and the Lord graciously raised up judges to save them from their enemies, 2:16-23. These judges were men of God who first of all had to judge the people of Israel. The judge made the people put away the false gods and straightened out any problems among the men of Israel.

The people of Israel could not win any victory as long as there was sin among them and they were divided among themselves. This is also true today. Christians cannot expect God to bless them and their service for Him if there is sin among them and if they are fighting with one another.

When the people had come back to Jehovah, the judge would lead them out to fight against their enemies and deliver them. We will see that many of the judges were also great soldiers.

However, the people often went back into sin even while the judge was still living, 2:17, and when he died, they started to worship other gods again even more than before, 2:19. Of course this made the Lord angry again and He told Israel that He would not drive out their enemies before them. This is the reason why people of many other nations lived in the land of Canaan besides the people of Israel.

This then is the sad story of the book of Judges. God's power was as great as it had been in the days of Joshua and Moses, but Israel turned away from Him again and again. They started to follow other gods in spite of all He had done for them. They repented when God punished them, but only for a short time.

We can learn many lessons from the Word of God, and Christians today should not have to go through such experiences again and again. God will bless us if we obey Him but He will have to take away these blessings if we disobey, until we repent and come back to Him.

OTHNIEL, EHUD, AND SHAMGAR,

chapter 3

4/6   The nations of Canaan continued to live in the land and were always fighting against Israel and causing trouble. This was part of God's plan so that the young men of Israel would learn to fight their enemies and trust the Lord. We see the names of eight nations in verses 1-6. The Philistines lived on the west side of Israel near the Sea. The Sidonians were north of the Philistines. The people of Israel lived among the other six nations. Some young people of Israel married the young men and girls of these nations and some of the older people served their gods, 3:6.

Christians have to fight against enemies too. A new Christian never wants to fall into sin again, but he soon finds that he has three enemies: the world, the flesh, and the devil. The Lord Jesus will put these enemies away for ever when He comes to take us to heaven. Until then we must learn to overcome them by faith and in the power of the Holy Spirit.

4/7 The Lord became angry when Israel soon began to serve the gods of their neighbors, so He allowed the king of Mesopotamia to rule over them for eight years, 3:7,8. Israel prayed to the Lord in their trouble and He raised up Othniel, the son of Caleb's brother, to deliver them. We already read about Othniel in Joshua 15:17 and Judges 1:13. Othniel had learned to fight and to trust the Lord when he was a young man, and now he was ready to deliver the people of God when they were in trouble. The Spirit of the Lord came on him and he defeated the king of Mesopotamia, 3:10. After that Israel lived in peace for forty years until Othniel died. This means that God kept Israel's enemies away from them as long as Othniel led them in the right way.

However, Israel soon went back into the ways of sin and this time God used Eglon, the king of Moab, to punish them. The Amalekites and the Ammonites helped Eglon in this, 3:13. The Amalekites had been enemies of Israel for many years, Exodus 17:8, but this is the first time the people of Ammon fought against them. Israel had to pay money to Eglon every year for eighteen years.

4/8 Finally Israel turned to the Lord and He raised up Ehud of the tribe of Benjamin to deliver them. Ehud thought of a brave plan. His name means *strong*, and he made a sword with two edges, about 18 inches (½ meter) long. The men of Moab did not have to work hard because of the money Israel had to pay them every year, and Eglon their king was fat and slow.

Ehud went to Moab with the money for that year. He paid the money to the king and then told him that he had a secret message for him, so the foolish king told his servants to go out of the room. Ehud did have a message from God for Eglon, a message of death. Ehud was different from most people in that his left arm was stronger than his right arm. No doubt the king thought Ehud would pull out a letter when he saw him reach under his clothes. Instead Ehud pulled out his sharp sword and drove it right through the body of the fat king. Then he left the room, locked the door after him and walked away.

4/9   After a while the king's servants went into the king's room and found him dead. In the meantime Ehud was able to escape and get back to Israel. He called together the armies of Israel and killed all the Moabites who tried to cross over the river, 10,000 of them.

After this great victory the people of Israel lived in peace for eighty years. However, even during this time the Philistines tried to fight against them, but Shamgar, another man of faith, killed 600 of them.

This chapter tells us about the first three judges of Israel who delivered them from their enemies. These judges are also called saviors and are pictures of our Lord Jesus Christ. We can be sure that our enemies will not leave us alone very long. We can also be sure that Christ will deliver us when we turn to Him. We will be safe only if we keep our eyes on the Lord. It is sad to see some Christians going on in sin. The Lord has taken away His joy from their hearts, but they refuse to come back to Him. The Lord would give them joy and victory once again if they would only repent and come back to Him.

TEST YOURSELF (Judges 1-3)

1. Explain one great difference between Joshua and Judges.

2. What are the main parts of the book of Judges?

3. The men of Judah cut off the thumbs and great toes of Adoni-Bezek. Was this right?

4. Why does the Holy Spirit tell us twice about Othniel and Achsah?

5. Name six tribes in Chapter 1 who did not have enough faith to do God's will. (You may look at your Bible for the answers.)

6. What happened at Bochim?

7. What was the work of a judge?

8. What was the great sin of the nations of Canaan?

9. What was Ehud's message from God to King Eglon?

10. In what way are the judges pictures of our Lord Jesus Christ?

Turn to page 114 to check your answers.

7 DEBORAH, BARAK, AND GIDEON

DEBORAH AND BARAK, chapters 4 and 5

4/10   The people of Israel fell into sin again after Ehud died. This time the Lord raised up Jabin, king of Canaan, and Sisera, the chief officer of his army, to punish Israel. Jabin and Sisera had 900 chariots made of metal in their army and they ruled over Israel for twenty years making life very unpleasant for them, 4:1-3.

God's people must put away all their sin before He will help them. In the time of the judges God usually raised up a man to teach His law to the people and to judge between those who had quarrels and problems. At this time there was no man willing and able to do this work, so God called a woman, Deborah, the prophetess, 4:4,5. When the people were cleansed of their sins they were ready to fight and to gain the victory over their enemies.

God commanded Deborah to call Barak and tell him to gather 10,000 men from the tribes of Naphtali and Zebulun. He promised to give this army victory over Sisera and King Jabin, 4:6,7. Barak was willing to obey the command of the Lord, but he wanted Deborah to go with him because she was a prophetess. Deborah promised to go but told Barak that the glory of the victory would not go to him but to a woman, 4:8-10. We shall see later that Deborah was speaking of Jael, not of herself.

Today those who serve the Lord know that they are constantly fighting against Satan and the forces of evil. Christian women can help the Lord's servants win these battles by praying for them. The Lord Jesus Christ will certainly honor these women when He comes back again.

4/11   In Exodus 18 we read about Jethro, the father of Moses' wife. Hobab was either another name for Jethro, or it was his son's name. Jethro visited Moses and the people of Israel at Mount Sinai, but then went back to his own land, Exodus 18:27. In Judges 1:16 and 4:11 we see that his descendants were called Kenites and that some of them lived among the people of Israel.

Sisera, the chief officer of the Canaanite army, heard that Barak had gathered 10,000 men together and went to fight with them. Deborah the prophetess encouraged Barak by telling him that the Lord would give them the victory over Sisera that day, 4:12-14. All Sisera's chariots were pulled by horses and each one had soldiers in it to fight against Israel, but Jehovah gave Israel the victory as He had promised and the Canaanites began to run away. Sisera himself got out of his chariot and ran away on foot. The soldiers of Israel caught up with the Canaanites and killed them all, 4:15,16.

4/12   Sisera ran from his army and came to the tent of Heber, the Kenite. Heber had made peace with the king of Hazor, but his wife Jael believed in Jehovah. She knew that Sisera had made life very difficult for God's people for twenty years and she decided to help them by killing him. She brought Sisera into her tent, made him feel comfortable, and gave him some milk when he asked her for a drink. Sisera was afraid the people of Israel would catch him and he told Jael to tell them that there was no one in the tent, 4:17-20. Then he fell asleep because he was very tired after the battle. Jael took a piece of wood, drove it through his head while he was sleeping, and killed him. Soon Barak arrived at Jael's tent looking for Sisera, and Jael showed him the dead body of his enemy, 4:21,22.

Deborah was a woman who knew the will of God. Barak was a brave fighter and a leader. Jael was a brave woman who wanted to help the people of God. God used them all to give Israel the victory that day, 4:23,24.

Today we follow the example of the Lord Jesus Christ who asked His Father to *forgive* His enemies, Luke 23:34, and we *pray* for our enemies instead of killing them, Matthew 5:44.

We can also help the people of God by praying for them. Our real enemies are not men and women but Satan and the wicked spirits who fight against God and His people,

Ephesians 6:12. God's servants would win greater victories today if we really prayed for them.

A song of praise, chapter 5

4/13   We should praise the Lord when He answers our prayers and gives us the blessings we asked for. This is what Deborah and Barak did in chapter 5 where they sang a song of praise to Jehovah because He had given them the victory, 5:1,2. Moses sang praise to the Lord when the Lord caused the Egyptians to die in the Red Sea, Exodus 15. His sister Miriam and the women joined in this song of praise, Exodus 15:20,21. Israel also sang a little song of praise in the desert, Numbers 21:17,18. Later Moses wrote another song to warn the people against falling into sin, Deuteronomy 32. In Ephesians 5:18,19 we read that we should be filled with the Spirit and should sing praises to God. In the future we will sing a new song of praise to the Lord together with all God's people, Revelation 5:9,10.

In our chapter Deborah and Barak called the kings of the world to listen while they gave glory to God, 5:3. Jehovah had delivered Israel from the Moabites of Mount Seir and the people of Edom when Israel first entered the land of Canaan, 5:4; Numbers 24:18; Deuteronomy 2:4,5. He had also shown His power at Mount Sinai where He gave the Law, 5:5; Exodus 19:18.

There was no good government in the land when Israel forsook God. In the days of Shamgar and Jael people were afraid to walk along the main roads because there were many robbers, 5:6. There was no judge to help the poor people before the time of Deborah, 5:7. Israel worshiped the gods of the people around them, the people who had taken all their spears and shields from them, 5:8. But many leaders of Israel were ready to help when the time came for Israel to be delivered, 5:9.

4/14   In verses 10 and 11 Deborah and Barak asked all the people, rich and poor, to tell how the Lord had given Israel the victory.

The time came when Deborah and Barak had to rise up in faith and Barak was called to lead away many prisoners, 5:12. The writer of Psalm 68 mentioned this verse in verse 18 and Paul used it in Ephesians 4:8 when speaking about the Lord Jesus Christ going back to heaven.

This shows us that Barak is a picture of the Lord Jesus Christ who gained the victory over all the forces of Satan.

4/15   Men from the tribes of Zebulun and Naphtali were the first ones to go and fight, 4:10. Later men from the tribes of Ephraim, Benjamin, and Issachar came to help them, 5:14,15. However the men of Reuben could not decide whether they should help in the battle or not, 5:15,16. The men of Gilead, Dan, and Asher were too busy with their own affairs, 5:17, but the men of Zebulun and Naphtali were not afraid to die for the Lord, 5:18.

The kings of Canaan came and fought against Israel, 5:19. It was really a spiritual war because Satan wanted Israel to go on in their sin, but God fought for them, 5:20. It seems that the river Kishon was especially full of water at that time because of very heavy rains and the waters of the river carried away many of Israel's enemies, 5:21. Others escaped on horses, 5:22.

4/16   The angel of the Lord put a curse on the people of Meroz because they refused to come to help the people of Jehovah, 5:23, but Jael received a special blessing, 5:24. The song tells how Sisera came to Jael and was killed, 5:25-27.

The women of Canaan expected their men to win the victory and to bring back slave girls and many beautiful things. The mother of Sisera began to wonder why her son stayed away so long, 5:28-30. But he never came back to her....

Deborah and Barak ended their song with a prayer that the enemies of Jehovah might be put to death but that all who love Him might be successful, 5:31.

After this victory the people of Israel followed the Lord for forty years without being attacked by any enemies.

GIDEON, chapters 6-8

4/17   There was peace in the land of Israel for forty years, but then the people fell into sin again. This time the Lord sent the Midianites to fight against Israel. They made life very difficult for Israel for seven years and destroyed the food Israel planted in their fields. Israel became very poor and finally the people turned back to Jehovah, 6:1-6.

Then the Lord spoke to them through a prophet whom He sent among them. The prophet told them that the Lord had delivered them from the Egyptians and the Canaanites and had commanded them not to worship the gods of the land, but they had not obeyed God, 6:7-10.

4/18   The best place to beat out grain is on top of a hill so that the wind can carry away the useless part of the grain. However the Midianites would soon see anyone who did so on top of a hill and would come quickly on their camels and take his grain. It was much harder to do this work in a valley or hollow, but this was the way Gideon did it so that the Midianites would not take away his family's food.

The angel of the Lord appeared to Gideon and told him that God was with him. Gideon found this difficult to understand because the people of Israel were having so much trouble, 6:13. He knew that the Lord had been able to deliver His people from Egypt, but felt that He had now turned against Israel. The Lord will always show His strength to anyone who is willing to admit that he is weak, so the angel told Gideon that in God's strength he would be able to deliver the people of Israel from the Midianites, in fact, God was sending him to do so, 6:14.

4/19   But Gideon was the youngest member of a small family in Manasseh and he was still thinking of his own weakness, 6:15. The Lord always gives us strength to do the things He tells us to do and so now He promised Gideon that He would be with him. Gideon wanted to believe this promise but he wanted to make sure that he had really understood correctly. He asked the Lord to give him a sign and the Lord agreed to wait until Gideon could prepare and bring a sacrifice. Gideon put the food of the sacrifice on a stone and the Lord caused fire to come out of the stone and burn up the sacrifice. Then suddenly Gideon could not see the angel any longer but he could still pray and the Lord told him that he would not die. So Gideon built an altar at that place which was still standing when the book of Judges was written, 6:16-24.

4/20   The Lord did these things to Gideon to teach him more of His ways and to prepare him for the great work He wanted him to do — to deliver Israel. First He wanted to test Gideon to see if he was brave and if he would obey the Lord and do something that was very difficult. He told Gideon to pull down the altar of the false god which belonged to his father, to cut down the trees which stood beside it, and to build in their place an altar of stones for Jehovah, 6:25,26. He also commanded Gideon to take his father's animal and offer it for a sacrifice to God.

Gideon found ten of his servants who were willing to help him in this difficult job but they were afraid that the other people might become angry, so they did the work at night instead of in the daytime.

It was not wrong for Gideon to pull down the altar *at night*. Many years later Nicodemus came to the Lord Jesus at night and the Lord was willing to talk to him and to show him how he could be born again, John 3:1-16. It is better to be afraid and obey than to be afraid and not obey.

The next morning the men of the town were very angry when they saw that the altar of the false god Baal had been destroyed, 6:28. They soon found out who had done this and told Joash, Gideon's father, that Gideon would have to die. Joash asked if they were really defending Baal. If this was the case, they were the ones who should be put to death, not Gideon. Baal should be able to look after himself if he was a real god. The men of the town listened to Joash and agreed to let Gideon live but Joash gave him a new name, Jerubbaal, 6:28-32. So we see that Gideon had been able to get his own servants, his father, and the men of the city to follow him.

4/21   Now the Midianites came into the land of Israel again to cause more trouble, 6:33. The Holy Spirit came on Gideon and he blew a trumpet to call the people of the town together. Then he sent messengers to call the men of four other tribes to come and help him fight against the Midianites, 6:33-35.

Even so Gideon was not quite sure that God had really chosen *him* to deliver Israel from their enemies, so he asked the Lord to give him another sign. He put a sheep skin on the ground at night and asked the Lord to let it become wet and to let the ground round about stay dry. The Lord answered this prayer and the next morning Gideon got enough water out of the sheep skin to fill a dish. The next night Gideon asked the opposite sign and again the Lord granted it, 6:36-40.

Gideon wanted to be very sure that the Lord had really sent him. We too should make very sure that we do only those things that God wants us to do. He has promised to show us His will if we want to know it. However the Lord will not lead us if we disobey any command of Scripture.

4/22   We have seen that Gideon had already learned a lot, but he was still not ready for the great victory which God wanted to give. He had an army of 32,000 men but the Midianites had so many soldiers that no one could count them. However God knew that the Israelites would become proud and take glory to themselves if God gave them the victory even though their army was much smaller than that of their enemies. So He told Gideon to send home all the men who were afraid, that is, those who did not have faith in God. There were only 10,000 Israelite soldiers left after Gideon obeyed this command, 7:2,3.

Moses had told the people of Israel that certain men should not go to war with the other soldiers, Deuteronomy 20:5-8. God will not give victory to those who do not follow Him completely or those who do not have faith. Their fear and their love for this world might spread to others, so it was better to send them home.

However even an army of 10,000 was too great and the Lord told Gideon to test the men in another way. They should all go down to the river for a drink of water. Most of the men of Israel got down on their knees so they could drink easily, but a few took a little water in their hands while keeping their eyes open and their heads up so that they would be able to see any enemies who might be approaching. It was not easy to drink water this way, but they were willing to put their own comfort second and the work of the Lord first. Only 300 men drank this way, but they were enough for God to give the victory to His people. The other 31,700 men were told to go back home because they were afraid or because they put their own comfort first, 7:4-8.

4/23   Gideon was willing to obey the Lord and send most of his men home. Now the Lord gave him another sign to strengthen his faith, 7:9-14. He told him to go down to the camp of the enemy at night together with one of his servants. Anyone would be more afraid than ever when he saw the large number of soldiers in the enemy's camp. However Gideon and his servant heard two of the men of Midian talking. One of them was telling the other about a dream he had had. In this dream he saw a piece of bread come into the camp of Midian and knock over a tent. The other soldier seemed to know the meaning of this dream. He said it meant that Gideon would get the victory over Midian.

Gideon praised the Lord when he heard this dream and its meaning, and returned to his own camp, 7:15-18. He told the 300 men to take courage because the Lord would give them the victory. He gave each soldier a trumpet and a lamp inside a clay pot and told them to follow his example.

> This is good advice for us also. We should keep our eyes on our Captain, the Lord Jesus Christ, and try to be like Him in everything.

4/24   About the middle of the night the three groups of men went to the camp of the enemy. Their lamps were in their pots and so the enemy watchmen did not see them coming. Suddenly Gideon and his men blew their trumpets and broke the pots. Usually there would be only one man with a trumpet and a lamp for many soldiers. The Midianites heard hundreds of trumpets and saw hundreds of lamps and probably thought that there were thousands of men attacking them. They were very much afraid, lost control of themselves, and started to kill one another, 7:22. Then they started to run away and Gideon called the men of three tribes to follow them, 7:23. He also called the men of Ephraim and they were able to catch two of the sons of the king, Oreb and Zeeb, and kill them, 7:24,25.

> In the New Testament we learn that we are the light of the world, Matthew 5:14, and that God has made His light shine in our hearts, 2 Corinthians 4:6. Perhaps Paul was thinking about Gideon and his 300 men when he wrote this verse. In verse 7 of the same chapter he went on to say that we have this light in clay pots, like the pots of Gideon's men. The light of the Gospel will not shine out from us to the people around us if we are always seeking for the riches and pleasures of this world. However the enemy will be overcome and the Lord's people blessed when we are like broken clay pots before the Lord.

Asaph also remembered these events when he wrote verse 11 of Psalm 83. Let us always remember these lessons.

Chapter 8

4/25   Sin was one reason why Israel could not overcome their enemies. Sometimes the tribes were quarreling and fighting among each other and often this was another reason why they were not able to gain the victory.

Ephraim felt that they were the chief tribe and this was partly true. Joshua was of the tribe of Ephraim and the men of Ephraim helped Barak in Judges 5:14. But now the men of Ephraim were jealous of Gideon and talked as if he should have called them first to go and fight against Midian, 8:1-3. Gideon replied softly and pointed out that they had already caught Oreb and Zeeb, sons of the king of Midian, but Gideon himself had no important prisoners at that time. The men of Ephraim had reaped the real harvest when they caught these important prisoners even though they came late. What the men of Abiezer or Gideon himself did was very small in comparison, like gathering the few grapes that remain on the vines after men have harvested the main crop, 8:2; 6:34.

> Jealousy always harms the work of the Lord, Romans 13:13; Galatians 5:20. Here we see that Gideon had learned another lesson: how to treat his jealous brothers. He did not become angry when they complained but answered them softly, Proverbs 15:1. The Lord Jesus Christ did the same thing, John 18:23. Christians too should learn to control their tongues. This is a sign that they are growing up in the things of the Lord, James 3:2.

There were some others who refused to help in the Lord's battle and were punished, 8:5-9. Gideon and his 300 men were very tired when they crossed the river Jordan, but they continued to follow the enemy, 8:4. Gideon asked the men of Succoth for some food for his army, but they refused to give him any. The men of Penuel also refused to help and Gideon warned them that he would punish them after he had won the victory.

Finally Gideon and his men caught Zebah and Zalmunna, the kings of Midian, and brought them back as prisoners while the rest of the army of Midian ran away in fear, 8:10-12.

4/26   On his way back Gideon took the elders of Succoth and beat them with thorny branches. Then he came to the city of Penuel and broke down the tower used by the watchmen, 8:13-17.

Zebah and Zalmunna had come into the land of Israel before and at that time they had killed Gideon's brothers at Tabor. Gideon asked them whom they had killed at Tabor and they tried to win Gideon's favor by saying he and his brothers looked like the sons of a king, hoping that Gideon might let them go free. Instead of that Gideon told his son Jether to kill them, but finally he killed them himself because Jether was afraid to do so, 8:18-21.

4/27   The men of Israel wanted Gideon to be their king because he had helped them to win a great victory. Gideon did the right thing when he refused this honor and said that God would rule over them. However he asked them to give him the earrings which they had taken from the men of Midian. The men of Israel agreed and Gideon used the metal to make an ephod. The ephod was part of the clothing of the high priest, Exodus 28:6, and was used to find out the will of God, 1 Samuel 23:9. Gideon should not have made an ephod and it caused him and his family and all Israel to sin, 8:22-27.

Gideon (also called Jerubbaal) had many wives and many sons. One of these sons was called Abimelech. The people of Israel followed the Lord as long as Gideon lived and there was peace in the land for forty years, 8:28. However after Gideon's death the people soon forgot Jehovah and the victory Gideon had won and started again to worship the gods of the nations around them.

We should be thankful for men of God who help us understand the Bible and who show us how we should live. However it might happen that sometimes we have no such teachers. In this case we should obey the Word of God anyway for we know that the Lord is able to keep His children who follow Him.

TEST YOURSELF (Judges 4-8)

1. What is necessary for God's people to do before He can bless them?

2. Deborah was a woman who knew God's will. She said the Lord would give victory to a woman. Who was this woman?

3. Name two women who sang songs of victory.

4. Why did Gideon beat out the grain in a wine press?

5. Why did the men say at first that Gideon should die?

6. Why did God send back the 31,700 men of Gideon's army?

7. What three signs did God give Gideon to strengthen his faith?

8. Why did the soldiers of Midian start to kill one another?

9. How did Gideon treat the men of Ephraim and Manasseh when they were jealous of him?

10. What was Gideon's sin?

Turn to page 115 to check your answers.

8 SEVEN JUDGES

ABIMELECH, chapter 9

4/28   Most of the judges of Israel were spiritual men who first judged Israel according to the Law of Jehovah and then delivered the people from their enemies. Abimelech however did not do either of these things. This chapter shows us how bad conditions were in the nation of Israel at this time.

Abimelech was a son of Gideon, but he lived with his mother at Shechem which was about 20 miles (30 kilometers) north of Ophrah. Shechem was a city of the Levites and a city of refuge, Joshua 20:7; 21:21. It should have been a place where the Levites taught God's Law and where men knew it and obeyed God. But in this chapter we do not read of any righteous people in Shechem.

First Abimelech asked the men of his mother's family to help him; he said it would be better for one man of their own town to rule over them than all 70 sons of Gideon. The people of Shechem were willing to follow Abimelech and they gave him seventy pieces of money which had been given to their god. The temple of Baal-berith was right in Shechem. Abimelech used this money to pay some wicked men to go with him to Ophrah to kill his own 70 brothers. The price of killing one man was only one piece of money. They killed 69 of Gideon's sons, (Abimelech's brothers) but the youngest one, Jotham, was able to get away. Then the men of Shechem made Abimelech their king, 9:1-6.

4/29   This is the first time a judge of Israel was called a king, but it is clear that God had not chosen Abimelech to be king over His people. The people had tried to make Gideon their king but Gideon refused to rule over Israel, 8:22,23.

Gideon's son Jotham had a message for the people of Shechem and went to Mount Gerizim. God had called Mount Gerizim the mountain of blessing, Deuteronomy 11:29; 27:12, and Joshua had used it for this purpose, Joshua 8:33. But now Jotham used it to curse these wicked men, 9:7-15. He told a story of trees as if they were men. He said the trees wanted to have a king to rule over them. They asked three different trees, the olive tree, the fig tree and the vine to be their king, but these all refused to be king over the trees because they were too busy with their own work to help others. These three trees were like Gideon, Jotham's father, who refused to be king. Finally the trees asked the bramble tree to be their king. The bramble tree is full of thorns. It does not bear any fruit and is of no use to anyone. The bramble tree was willing to be king over the trees if they really wished him to be their king. However fire would burn up the trees if they named him king without really wanting him, 9:15.

This is the way Jotham felt about the men of Shechem. He asked if they really did the right thing when they made Abimelech to be their king. If not, he asked God to send trouble to Abimelech and to the men of Shechem, 9:16-21. He also wanted them to remember that his father had saved them from the Midianites but in return they had killed 69 of Gideon's sons on one stone.

4/30   For three years all went well, but then God sent trouble between Abimelech and the men of Shechem, 9:22-25. Abimelech knew that some of the men of Shechem robbed travelers but he could not or would not stop them.

Then a man called Gaal moved into Shechem while Abimelech was away. He got some of the people to follow him and to speak against
5/1   Abimelech, 9:26-29. Zebul, the ruler of the city, heard about this and told Abimelech, 9:30-33. Abimelech came back to Shechem with all his men and Gaal saw them as they got close to the city. Zebul told Gaal he was just seeing the shadows of the mountains, but Gaal knew they were men coming to fight against him. He went out to fight but many of
5/2   his men were wounded and ran back into the city, 9:34-41. Zebul made Gaal and his family leave, but the next day Abimelech and his army came again and killed the men of Shechem who were in the fields as well as those who were in the city. They destroyed all the houses in the city and then spread salt over the whole area so that nothing would grow on the ground, 9:42-45.

Many of the people of Shechem had gone into a strong tower thinking they would be safe in it. However Abimelech and his men piled a great deal of wood around the tower and set the tower on fire and another thousand men and women died there, 9:46-49.

5/3   Perhaps Abimelech thought he could destroy the people of Shechem and not be judged by God himself. He went to Thebez and there too the people ran into a tower to protect themselves against him and his army. Abimelech thought he would burn this tower as he had done in Shechem, but a woman threw a large stone out of the tower which fell on Abimelech's head. Abimelech knew he would die very soon but he did not use his last hours to repent of his sins before God. Instead he told his helper to kill him with a sword because he did not want people to say that a woman had killed him, 9:50-54. When he was dead the men of Israel stopped fighting each other and went back home. So we scc that God punished both Abimelech and the men who helped him kill his brothers.

We can be sure that God will punish all those who do wrong. Christians should be careful not to follow any leader who teaches them things which are not in the Word of God. All believers should understand what the Bible teaches so that they will know immediately when someone comes and teaches them something different. In this chapter the men of Shechem could have saved their own lives by listening to the advice of Jotham and putting Abimelech out.

JEPHTHAH, chapters 10-12

5/4   Abimelech was not a good judge and another judge, Tola, delivered Israel after his death. Tola belonged to the tribe of Issachar, but he lived in Ephraim and judged Israel for 23 years, 10:1,2.

After Tola, Jair judged Israel for 22 years. He lived in the land of Gilead on the east side of the Jordan River. He had 30 sons who rode on 30 donkeys which showed that they too had authority as judges, 10:3-5. We do not know anything else about Tola and Jair except that they kept the people following the Lord at least in part.

Soon the people of Israel started to sin again and to serve the gods of the nations around them. The Lord became very angry. He raised up the Philistines and the Ammonites to punish His people. The people of Gilead had to serve the Ammonites for 18 years, and after that, the Ammonites crossed the river Jordan to fight against the other tribes of Israel, 10:6-9.

5/5   Finally the people of Israel were willing to come back to Jehovah. The Lord told them that He had already delivered them many times but that they still continued to serve other gods. So God told them to continue to pray to these false gods whom they had chosen. The people of Israel knew that only Jehovah could deliver them and so they put away all the false gods among them. The Lord saw that they had really repented and He got ready to help them, 10:10-16.

The people of Israel gathered together to fight when the Ammonites came up to attack them, but they did not have anyone to lead them. However the men of Gilead agreed to accept as their leader anyone who would go to fight against the Ammonites, 10:17,18.

Chapter 11

5/6   Jephthah had been leading an unhappy life. He was a brave fighter, but his brothers did not allow him to live with them because of his mother. So Jephthah and his men robbed other people in order to get what they needed, 11:1-3.

Now the men of Gilead sent someone to call Jephthah because they wanted him to be their leader when they went to fight against the Ammonites. At first Jephthah refused to come and help them, but he changed his mind when the people of Gilead promised that he would be their ruler if he would fight for them. So Jephthah went back with those who had come to call him and he began to follow the Lord, 11:4-11.

5/7   It is good to know that God is always ready to help His people if they truly repent of their sins. He can use sinful people if they really turn to Him, and Jephthah became a man of God even though he had had a bad start.

First Jephthah tried to talk and reason with the king of the Ammonites, but the king refused to listen to him, 11:12-28. The king accused Israel of taking some of the land belonging to the Ammonites and said that now the Ammonites wanted it back again, 11:13. This was a piece of land which had the river Arnon as its southern border, the Dead Sea and the river Jordan as its border on the west, and the river Jabbok on the north.

Then Jephthah sent a message to the king of the Ammonites to explain what had really taken place. The Ammonites and the Moabites were all descendants of Lot, Genesis 19:37,38. Israel had asked the king of Edom permission to go through his land when they came from Egypt on their way to the land of Canaan, 11:17; Numbers 20:18-21. However the king of Edom did not allow them to go through his land, so they had to go around the land of Edom and the land of Moab, Numbers 21:4,11.

5/8   Israel had then sent a message to Sihon, king of the Amorites who were descendants of Canaan and Ham, 11:19; Genesis 10:6,15,16. The Amorites had taken the land between these three rivers from the people of Moab, Numbers 21:26, but the Lord gave Israel the victory when Sihon, king of the Amorites, came out to fight against them, Numbers 21:21-25.

5/9   So Jehovah had given this land to Israel and the Ammonites should be content with what Chemosh, their god had given them, 11:24. This does not mean that Jephthah thought Chemosh was equal to Jehovah. The king of Moab had never tried to take back this land from Israel and for 300 years Ammon had not demanded it, so why should they start now, 11:25-27? In verse 27 Jephthah called on Jehovah to judge this affair. The king of the Ammonites did not pay any attention to Jephthah's message and refused to call his army back home, 11:28.

5/10   Then the Spirit of the Lord came on Jephthah and he won a great victory, 11:29-33. Jephthah had promised the Lord that he would give back to the Lord whatever came out of the door of his house to meet him when he came back from the battle victoriously. He came home with great joy, but his joy was changed to sorrow because his daughter was the first one to come out of the house to meet him. This girl was Jephthah's only child and Jephthah tore his clothes to show his sorrow when he saw her. Jephthah's daughter did not ask her father to break the promise he had made to the Lord but she requested that she might have two months with her girl friends before he fulfilled his promise.

5/11   At the end of the two months Jephthah did what he had
          promised to the Lord. Some people think that he killed
his daughter and offered her as a burnt offering, 11:31. This was
a common custom among the Canaanites and the Ammonites,
but the Lord specially commanded Israel not to do this,
Leviticus 18:21; Deuteronomy 12:31; 18:10. Jephthah knew the
Law of Moses even though his mother was a sinful woman. We
should note that verse 31 could mean *or I will offer him for an
offering*. It may be that Jephthah sent his daughter to serve the
Lord at the tabernacle without getting married. Some years later
Samuel's mother brought her little son to the tabernacle to serve
the Lord, 1 Samuel 1:28. In the New Testament we are told not
to make such promises as Jephthah had done but to present our
bodies to the Lord as a living sacrifice, Romans 12:1.

Chapter 12

5/12   This was not the end of Jephthah's trouble. We saw in
          8:1-3 that the men of Ephraim were jealous of Gideon,
but Gideon spoke softly to them and their anger passed away.
Now the men of Ephraim asked Jephthah why he had not called
them, and said they might burn down his house with him in it.
This was a custom of the Philistines, 14:15. Jephthah answered
that he did call them, but that they had refused to come, 12:2,3.
The men of Ephraim fought against the Gileadites but the
Gileadites won the victory.

     The men of Ephraim tried to cross the river Jordan to
get home but the Gileadites stopped each man and asked him if
he was an Ephraimite. Of course the man said "no"; he was
then told to say the word *Shibboleth*. Those who could not say
this word properly did belong to the tribe of Ephraim and were
put to death by the men of Gilead; 42,000 men died at that
time, 12:4-6. The men of Gilead killed them because the way
they said *Shibboleth* proved that they were from Ephraim, their
enemies.

     Jephthah continued to judge Israel for six years before
he died, 12:7.

God's people are sometimes troubled by those on the out-side who do not belong to them, and sometimes by other Christians. Jephthah was able to gain the victory over the Ammonites, but after that he had trouble with another tribe of Israel. The apostle Paul also had trouble from outside (unbe-lievers) and inside (false friends), 2 Corinthians 11:24-26. In the book of Judges we find that often the judge had to settle the quarrels of the people of Israel before he could expect them to unite to fight against their enemies. Again and again Satan succeeds in stopping the work of God by making Christians quarrel among themselves.

5/13   In the second part of the chapter we have a short account of three judges, Ibzan, 12.8-10; Elon, 12:11,12; and Abdon, 12:13-15. Two of these men must have had many wives because they also had many children, see verses 9 and 14. We do not read anywhere else in the Bible about them, but they served the Lord and so their names were recorded in this chapter. We can be sure that God will remember every-thing we do for Him, 1 Corinthians 15:58.

TEST YOURSELF (Judges 9-12)

1. Would you say Abimelech was a brave and a good man?

2. How many sons of Gideon were killed?

3. Why did Jotham tell the story about the trees?

4. Who killed Abimelech?

5. Why did God tell Israel to pray to their own gods, 10:14?

6. Why did Jephthah at first refuse to be leader of Gilead?

7. Why did Jephthah try to reason with the king of the Ammonites?

8. Why did Jephthah give his daughter to the Lord?

9. In what way was Jephthah different from Gideon?

10. Why did the Gileadites make people say "Shibboleth"?

Turn to page 116 to check your answers.

9 SAMSON

5/14   Samson is the last of the judges we read about in this book. Chapter 13 tells about his good start in life, chapters 14 and 15 tell of his great acts, and chapter 16 tells about Delilah and Samson's death.

Once again Israel fell into sin and the Lord allowed the Philistines to rule over them for forty years, but He began to prepare a deliverer for them long before the forty years were over.

First of all the angel of the Lord came to a faithful woman of the tribe of Dan. This woman and her husband had no children at that time, but the angel told her that she would have a son who would be a Nazirite to God from the time he was born. God would use this son to deliver Israel from the Philistines.

What kind of person could be a Nazirite? Any Israelite who decided to set aside part of his life for the work of the Lord could be a Nazirite. The laws of the Nazirite are found in Numbers 6. He was not allowed to drink wine or strong drink nor to touch a dead body, vs. 3,6, and he could not cut his hair. It is a shame for a man to have long hair, 1 Corinthians 11:14, but the Nazirite was willing to have long hair for a while in order to please the Lord.

The angel also told the woman that she should not drink wine nor eat anything unclean. In Leviticus 11 there is a long list of animals, birds, and fish which were unclean.

The woman told her husband that a man of God had talked with her and had informed her that she would have a son who would be a Nazirite to God from the time he was born until the day he died. However the angel had *not* said that the boy would *always* be a Nazirite and we will see later that Samson broke the law of the Nazirite. The angel had told the woman that her son would begin to deliver Israel, but it seems that she could not quite believe this because she did not tell her husband about it.

5/15   Manoah asked the Lord to send the man again and the angel appeared once more to the woman as she sat in the field. The woman called her husband and Manoah asked the angel how they should raise the boy. The angel repeated what the boy's mother should and should not do, 13:8-14.

In the book of Genesis the Lord sometimes appeared to men in the form of an angel, Genesis 16:7; 22:11. John 1:18 tells us that no man has ever seen God, but that the Son of God has made Him known to men. From this verse we understand that it was really the Son of God who appeared to men in Old Testament times.

5/16   Manoah wanted to get some food ready for this wonderful Person who had brought them such good news. The angel said that he would not eat the food but that Manoah could bring it as a burnt offering to the Lord. Manoah asked the angel what his name was but the angel told him only that his name was wonderful. This also makes us think of the Lord Jesus Christ, Isaiah 9:6. Manoah put his offering on the rock, a flame went up from the rock, and the angel of the Lord went up in the flame.

Here we get a view of the God who is wonderful, whose name is Wonderful, and who does wonderful things. He made the earth and created all men, but even more wonderful is the fact that He saved us from sin and prepares us for heaven.

Manoah did not know the truths of the New Testament and he was very much afraid thinking God would kill him and his wife because they had seen Him. His wife had more faith and reminded her husband that God had accepted their offering and had told them that they would have a son, 13:21-23. Finally the baby was born and the parents called him Samson. The Lord blessed him and the Spirit of the Lord began to come on him when he grew up.

SAMSON'S WONDERFUL POWER, chapters 14,15

5/17   Samson knew that the Philistines were the enemies of God's people and that God wanted him to deliver Israel. He tried to do so, but not in the way God wanted him to do it. Many years before this, Moses had also tried to deliver Israel in his own way, but he had to learn that he must do God's work in the way and at the time God wanted him to do it, Exodus 2:11-15; 3:1-10.

Samson went down to Timnath and decided to marry one of the Philistine girls. His parents told him he should marry a girl of Israel, but Samson would not listen to this, 14:1-4. He went again to Timnath and met a young lion when he got close to the town. Samson had nothing in his hand to defend himself against this wild animal, but by the help of the Holy Spirit he was able to kill it. He did not tell his parents what he had done but went on to talk to the young woman and found that she pleased him, 14:5-7.

Samson did not ask the Lord if it was *His* will for him to marry this girl. Many young people today make a terrible mistake when they get married to someone who is not a true Christian. We must ask the Lord to show us His will in every important decision we have to make.

5/18   A few days later Samson found that bees had entered the dead body of the lion and had left honey there. Samson was not allowed to touch a dead body because he was a Nazirite, but he wanted the honey very much. He took some out with his hands, ate some of it himself and gave some to his father and mother without telling them where he got it, 14:8,9. Here again we see Samson pleasing himself and disobeying God's commands.

Samson's father went down to Timnath to see the woman whom Samson wanted to marry, and Samson made a feast according to the custom of the young men in those days. At the feast Samson thought of a way to get some clothes from the thirty young Philistine men who came to his feast. He asked them a hard question and promised to give each of them two pieces of clothing if any one could tell him the answer. However each of them would have to give him two pieces of clothing if they could not think of the answer. Samson's question was about the lion and the honey which he found in the lion's dead body. A lion eats other animals and even men, but Samson had gotten something to eat from the lion. Also a lion is very strong and honey is very sweet.

5/19   The Philistines were not able to get the answer for three days, so they went to Samson's wife before the feast was over and told her to ask him what the answer was and then tell it to them. They said that they would burn her to death in her father's house if she did not help them. So all during the feast, the woman kept on asking Samson what the answer was. She kept on weeping and telling him that he did not really love her until finally Samson could not stand it any longer and told her the answer. She told the answer to the Philistines but of course Samson realized that they had found the answer only through his wife, 14:18.

Now Samson had to get the clothes which he had promised to give to the young men, so he went to Ashkelon, another Philistine city, and there he killed thirty men and took their clothes. He was very angry about what had happened and went home again without his wife who was then given to another man.

The Lord was willing to help Samson in these things but this does not mean that Samson was doing what was right. God wanted to punish the Philistines to save His people, but Samson did it in a way which was not according to God's plan. So we see that God does sometimes use a servant who is not perfect. However we should try to do God's work according to His will and in His power.

Chapter 15

5/20   Samson did not know that his wife had been given to another man and so after a while he took a gift and went to see her. Her father told him that she was married to someone else, but said that Samson could marry her sister instead. Samson did not want to marry the sister and so he decided to revenge himself on the Philistines. He caught 300 foxes and tied the tails of every two foxes together with a torch between their tails. Then he set the torches on fire and let the foxes loose in the fields of the Philistines. The foxes ran off in all directions and spread fire everywhere they went. This destroyed the crops of the Philistines which meant that many people would not have enough to eat that year. The olive trees also burned down which was still worse. The Philistines could plant more grain the following year, but olive trees do not bear fruit for many years after they are planted, 15:1-5.

The Philistines were very angry when they found out that Samson had done this and that he had done it because his wife had been given to another man. They came and burned Samson's wife and her father. This made Samson more angry still and he killed many Philistines, 15:6-8.

5/21   Then the Philistines told the men of Judah to arrest Samson. The men of Judah did not want any trouble with the Philistines, so their rulers and 3000 men went to get Samson. They promised Samson that they would not kill him themselves but would only bind him and bring him to the Philistines, 15:9-13.

5/22   The Philistines shouted when they saw Samson tied with ropes, but the Holy Spirit came on Samson and he broke the ropes. He had nothing in his hands to fight with, but he found a bone of a dead animal and killed a thousand men with it in the strength of the Lord. He sang a little song of victory and then threw the bone away, 15:14-17.

After all this Samson was so thirsty that he thought he would die. He prayed to God about this and the Lord provided water for him from a spring. Altogether Samson judged Israel for twenty years, 15:18-20.

In this chapter we see that the people of Israel were willing to be the servants of the Philistines, but Samson tried to find a good reason to attack them. He had a little faith and the Lord saw this faith and gave him great strength to overcome his enemies.

SAMSON AND DELILAH, chapter 16

5/23   Samson still had not learned to leave the Philistine women alone. He went down to Gaza, a large Philistine city, and went in to a sinful woman, a prostitute. The men of the city knew where he was and waited for him hoping to catch him in the morning. They had locked the gate of the city so that he would not be able to escape. However Samson got up in the middle of the night, pulled up the doors of the gate and the two posts and carried them to Hebron about 35 miles (56 kilometers) away. No doubt Samson had begun to realize that he should not be among the sinful Philistines and had repented before the Lord, so the Lord gave him back his old strength and enabled him to escape, 16:1-3.

The next time, however, Samson was not able to save himself. He fell in love with another Philistine woman named Delilah. This woman was willing to act as if she loved Samson in order to earn 5,500 pieces of silver. There were five lords of the Philistines, 3:3, and each one promised her 1,100 pieces of silver. Samson was willing to give up his spiritual power as the savior and judge of Israel in order to be with this wicked woman.

Delilah asked Samson to tell her what made him so strong. Perhaps Samson really thought he would become weak if they tied him up. Delilah brought the Philistines into another room, then tied up Samson as he had said. However Samson got up and broke his bonds quite easily when he heard that the Philistines were there to make him their prisoner, 16:4-9.

5/24   The second time Samson told Delilah that he would not be able to escape if they bound him with new cords, but again he broke the cords like string, 16:10-12.

The third time he told her he would not be able to get away if she tied the hair of his head right into the cloth she was making. Delilah did this while Samson was sleeping, and then woke him up, but he pulled away the whole cloth-making machine.

5/25   We cannot understand why Samson did not leave Delilah. He should have realized what Delilah was trying to do, but instead he stayed on and fell into her trap. Delilah said Samson did not really love her. We might ask if she really loved him! She kept asking him day after day why he was so strong until finally he told her. He said he was so much stronger than other men because he was separated to God. He was a Nazirite and the sign of his separation was his long hair.

Delilah realized that Samson had at last told her the whole truth and so she called the Philistines to come once more with their money. She put Samson to sleep, called someone to cut off his hair and then woke him up by saying the Philistines were there. Samson thought he would be able to get away as before, but now his great strength was gone.

Sometimes a Christian falls into sin, but still tries to go on with his work for the Lord. He soon discovers that he no longer has the power he needs to serve the Lord as he should.

This time the Philistines made Samson their prisoner and put out his eyes. Then they bound him with chains, took him to Gaza and made him work in the prison. The mighty Samson had killed a thousand of his enemies at one time, but now he was blind and weak! But his hair began to grow again, 16:22.

5/26   The Philistines did not know or believe that Samson was now weak because he had sinned. Instead they gave thanks to Dagon, their false god, for having helped them catch their enemy, 16:23,24. Then they called Samson so that he might amuse them.

The people were all gathered in a large building which was supported by two main pillars. Samson asked the boy who led him to help him touch the pillars, 16:26,27. Then he prayed to the Lord and asked Him to make him strong just once more. Samson was willing to give his own life in order to gain one last great victory over his enemies, 16:28,29. He pulled over the two pillars and the whole temple was weakened and fell down. Many, many people were killed—even more than Samson had killed during his whole life. Then his brothers came, took his body and buried him at home.

Samson was brought up as a Nazirite, separated to Jehovah, and it is sad to note that he did only part of what he could have done for the Lord. The Holy Spirit *began* to move him, and he *began* to deliver Israel, 13:5,25. But then he started to associate with the people of the world instead of remaining separated to the Lord. Many Christians today refuse God's will by marrying someone who is not a true believer. Indeed many of us serve the Lord with only half of our hearts and lives and with the other half we follow the world. We want to serve God but we also want the things of this world. We are like those in the church of Laodicea, neither hot nor cold, Revelation 3:15.

Samson's eyes led him away from the Lord. With those eyes he looked at a beautiful Philistine girl, and wanted her for himself. Finally the Philistines put his eyes out and he returned in heart to the Lord. These things should be a warning to us. Let us learn from the Bible, serve the Lord, and remain separate from the world.

TEST YOURSELF (Judges 13-16)

1. What was a Nazirite?

2. Why did the Lord tell Manoah's wife not to drink any wine?

3. Why was Manoah afraid?

4. In what way was Samson like Moses?

5. Why was it wrong for Samson to eat the honey he found in the lion's body?

6. Why did Samson tie 300 foxes together two by two by their tails?

7. Why did the men of Judah give Samson over to his enemies?

8. Why did Delilah act as if she loved Samson?

9. Why did Samson become weak when Delilah cut his hair?

10. In what way was Samson like the church of Laodicea?

Turn to page 117 to check your answers.

10 SIN IN ISRAEL

5/27   In chapters 17 to 21 we read about two events which show the
terrible condition of Israel between the times of Joshua and
Samuel. In these five chapters we read four times that there was no king
in Israel, 17:6; 18:1; 19:1; 21:25. Often the people did not even have a
good judge and they quickly forgot the Law of Jehovah. In chapters 17
and 18 we read about Micah and his priest. Then chapters 19 to 21 show
that there was serious sin in the land.

MICAH AND HIS PRIEST, chapters 17, 18

In chapter 17 we read of a woman of the tribe of Ephraim who
had 1,100 pieces of silver. Someone stole the money from her and she
put a curse on the person who had taken it. Later her son Micah confessed that he was guilty of taking the money. He told his mother that he
would return it to her and she then changed the curse into a blessing. She
decided to give the money to the Lord and thought it would be good to use
some of it to make two silver images. Perhaps she did not know the second commandment, Exodus 20:4, or she refused to obey it.

Then Micah made a little house for the images, as well as an
ephod and *teraphim*. Gideon had also made an ephod, 8:27, but we noted
that he should not have done so. Teraphim were images which people
worshiped in their homes, Genesis 31:19. People were breaking God's
Law when they had these teraphim in the house and worshiped them,
1 Samuel 15:23; 2 Kings 23:24. Micah was also breaking God's Law
when he made his son a priest, 17:5, because only the sons of Aaron
were to be priests, Exodus 28:1. Later on God punished other men who
tried to act as priests, 2 Chronicles 26:16-21.

In the days of Micah there was no king in Israel and everyone
did what he wanted to do, 17:6. This verse explains many things we read

in the book of Judges. A good king would not have allowed the people to worship idols, but those who believed in Jehovah obeyed the commands of the Law even before Israel had a king.

5/28   Soon Micah was able to find a Levite who was willing to be his priest, 17:7-13. Micah paid this man and thought the Lord would bless him if he had a priest who was a Levite. According to the Law only the sons of Aaron were to be priests, not all Levites. This young man should have known that Jehovah had commanded His people not to make images and therefore he should not have stayed with Micah to be his priest. However he wanted the money and so he stayed.

Today also God's servants sometimes do what is not right because they get paid for it, Titus 1:11. We are not surprised therefore at Paul's words that the love of money is a source of all kinds of evil, 1 Timothy 6:10.

Chapter 18

5/29   Chapter 18 tells us about part of the tribe of Dan moving to the north and taking with them Micah's images and his false priest.

In Joshua 19:40-48 we saw that the tribe of Dan received eighteen cities but they felt this was not enough for them because they were not able to drive the Amorites out of their territory. They should have asked the Lord to give them the necessary strength to overcome the Amorites, but instead they sent five men to the north to look for a town which did not have a strong army to protect it.

The five men came to the house of Micah and talked to his false priest. The priest told them that Micah paid him a good salary for being his priest. He also told the men of Dan that God would bless their journey. Could he, a false priest, really say what the Lord would do for the men of Dan? The five men did succeed in their journey, but this does not prove that God spoke through the false priest. In Deuteronomy 13:1-5 we see that a false prophet sometimes tells the truth about the future, but that he should be put to death if he tells people to follow other gods, and not Jehovah.

The five men found the town of Laish (called Leshem in Joshua 19:47) and saw that the people of the town were wealthy and had no one to protect them from their enemies. So the men of Dan returned home and told the other men of their tribe that they should go and take this city, 18:7-10.

5/30   Six hundred men started out to go to Laish. They first came to the house of Micah and the five men told the others that there were images and an ephod in Micah's house, 18:11-14. The men of Dan decided to steal these images and the five men just walked in and took them. Micah's priest asked them what they were doing but they told him to go with them and be the priest for a whole family in the tribe of Dan. The priest was happy to go along with them for he knew he would receive more money working for a large family than for just one man, 18:15-20.

6/1   Micah called together the men who lived near him and hurried after the men of Dan. The Danites acted as if they did not know why Micah should come after them. Micah accused them of having taken away his priest and the gods he had made, but the men of Dan told him to be quiet or they would kill him. Micah saw that they were too strong for him and those with him, so he went back home, 18:21-26.

The men of Dan came to Laish, killed all the people and burned the city. Then they rebuilt the city, called it Dan, set up the images and put the priest in charge of them. Now we learn that the priest's name was Jonathan and that he was a grandson of Moses. He was called a young man, 17:7, so these things must have taken place soon after Joshua's death. Jonathan's sons and grandsons were priests in the tribe of Dan for many years. This was a sin against God because it was not according to His Law.

These two chapters show that Israel was in a terrible condition spiritually at that time. A man of Ephraim thought the Lord would bless him because he made silver images and got a false priest. The men of Dan also thought these images were of great value and that the priest would be a help to them, so they stole the images and offered the priest more money. Micah protested about this but they threatened to kill him if he did not keep quiet. It is sad to think that the people of Israel could get so far away from the Lord in such a short time. They had the Law of God and the true priests, the sons of Aaron, to guide them even though they did not have a king or judge at that time. May these two chapters be a warning to us!

It is just as easy for Christians today to get away from the Lord, but there is absolutely no excuse for it. We have the Word of God in our hands and the Holy Spirit in our hearts to help us follow the Lord closely.

THE LEVITE AND HIS WOMAN, chapters 19-21

6/2   Here we have another story of a Levite, but this one did not accept a salary in order to do the work of a priest. He lived in Ephraim but took a woman from Bethlehem to live with him without marrying her. After some time the woman left him and went back to her father's house but four months later the Levite followed her in order to bring her back. The woman's father was glad to see him and the Levite stayed there for several days, 19:1-9.

6/3   Finally he and the woman got ready to leave, but the woman's father tried to persuade them to stay one more night. It was already late in the afternoon, but the Levite decided that they must get on their way. They came to a city of Jebus in the land of Judah. This city was inhabited by the Jebusites whom the people of Judah had not been able to drive out, Joshua 15:63. The Levite did not want to stay with these strangers, so they went on to Gibeah, another 7 miles (11 kilometers) further. The city of Gibeah was also in the land of Judah, but had been given to the tribe of Benjamin, Joshua 15:57; 18:28. The Levite thought that the people of Benjamin would be kinder to them than the Jebusites, but no one would receive them when they arrived in Gibeah after the sun had set.

The Scriptures teach us to be kind to strangers and to help people in need, Romans 12:13.

Finally an old man came along and talked to them. He belonged to the tribe of Ephraim but was living at that time in Gibeah. The Levite told him that they had enough food for themselves and the animals, but that they would like a place to sleep for the night. The old man invited them to stay with him and said he would provide them with everything
6/4   they needed, 19:16-21. However, while they were eating together, wicked men of the town came to the house and told the old man to bring out his visitor because they wanted to commit sin and humble him. The old man tried to reason with them and even offered them his

daughter and the woman of the Levite, but they would not listen to him. Finally the Levite made his woman go out and they attacked her all night. At last they left her alone and she fell down at the door of the house.

This is one of the saddest events we read about in the Bible. The men of Gibeah acted like the men of Sodom had done many years before, Genesis 19. The men of Sodom came to Lot's house at night and tried to make him bring out his visitors to them. Lot refused but offered them his two daughters instead, but they were not satisfied. Lot's visitors were angels and they finally made the men of Sodom blind. The next day Sodom was destroyed by fire from heaven.

The men of Gibeah knew what had happened in Sodom, but still they followed the example of the men of Sodom. Even true Christians can fall into the worst sins if they get away from the Lord.

In the morning the Levite was ready to continue his journey when he saw his woman lying at the door and found that she was dead. He was sorry and angry for he had wanted to take her back to his home, even though she had fallen into sin. We cannot understand why he had given her to the wicked men of the town but now he realized that they must be punished, 19:27-30.

He brought the dead body of the woman home, cut it into twelve pieces and sent these throughout all the land of Israel. In this way the whole nation heard what had happened and they all felt that nothing as terrible as this had ever happened before.

Chapter 20

6/5   The people of Israel felt very badly when they heard about this terrible event. From all parts of Israel 400,000 men met together at Mizpah and asked the Levite to tell them what had happened. He told them that the men of Gibeah had planned to kill him and that they did kill the woman with whom he was living, 20:1-7.

6/6   The men of Israel knew that God would not bless them if they did not punish the men of Gibeah for this sin. They told ten men of every hundred to go and get food for the rest, 20:8-11. Then they sent a message to the tribe of Benjamin telling them to turn over these wicked men of Gibeah to them. The men of Benjamin did not think that the men of Gibeah had done anything wrong for which they should be punished, so 26,000 men of Benjamin gathered together to fight against the other tribes who had many more men and who also had God on their side. The men of Israel asked the Lord which tribe should go first to fight against the Benjamites and the tribe of Judah was chosen, as in 1:2.

6/7   The battle started and it seemed as if the men of Benjamin were stronger than the others. The other tribes had more men than Benjamin and so were too confident before the battle, but now they cried to the Lord with tears and asked if they should really fight against their brothers, 20:19-23. The next day the men of Israel were a little more successful, but the men of Benjamin were still stronger than they, and 18,000 men died. Then the whole army of Israel went to Bethel to pray to the Lord and offer sacrifices. Phinehas the priest was there with them as well as the Ark of God. Again the Lord told them to attack the men of Benjamin and promised to give them the victory the next day, 20:24-28.

6/8   No doubt the people of Israel remembered what Joshua had done at Ai, Joshua 8:4-8. They used a similar plan and placed some of the men behind the city of Gibeah. Then the main army started to fight against the Benjamites as before and the men of Benjamin expected to win again. At first Israel ran away as before, but then they sent 10,000 of the bravest men to fight against Benjamin. These men killed most of the Benjamites before the day was over, 20:29-36.

6/9   Verses 37 to 48 give us more details about that day. The men of Israel who were hiding behind the city rushed into the city and set it on fire. The main army turned around to fight against Benjamin when they saw smoke rising from the city. Some of the men tried to escape, but only 600 were able to get away.

It is always sad to see people fighting against those they love, but our love for God must be greater than our love for our brothers. Those who have sinned should confess their sin and should be punished if they refuse to do so. Today God does not want Christians to kill people who fall into sin, but these people should be put out of the church until they confess their sins. We need the power of the Lord for these things, 1 Corinthians 5:4,5,11.

Here in Judges 19 and 20 Israel had to judge the men of Gibeah and the men of Benjamin but they should not have destroyed all the women and children as well. We might note that in chapter 18 the men of Dan were *not* punished for the terrible sin of setting up idols and worshiping them.

Chapter 21

6/10 So the tribe of Benjamin was punished for the sin of the men of Gibeah, but afterwards the men of Israel were very sorry because one of the tribes of Israel had been destroyed. There were only 600 men of Benjamin left and no women or children. The men of Israel had sworn two things before they went to fight against Benjamin. They swore that:

1) they would not allow any man from Benjamin to marry their daughters.

2) they would kill any man of Israel who did not come to help them in the war against Benjamin, 21:1-7.

6/11 They soon found out that no one had come from Jabesh-gilead to help them fight against Benjamin, so they sent 12,000 men to kill all the people of Jabesh-gilead except all the girls who had never been married. They wanted these girls to become the wives of the men of Benjamin who were left so that the tribe would not be completely destroyed. This plan was partly successful and 400 young girls were found for the men of Benjamin, 21:8-12.

6/12 Then the men of Israel sent messengers to the men of Benjamin to tell them they could come back. They gave to each of 400 men of Benjamin a wife, but 200 men were still left without wives, 21:13-15.

6/13 So the elders of Israel had to find wives for the 200 men. They had sworn that none of the other tribes would give Benjamin their daughters for wives and they knew that God would judge them if they did not keep this promise. So they told the 200 men of Benjamin to catch wives for themselves from among the girls of Shiloh when they came out to dance at the feast. Ordinarily this would cause even more trouble, but the elders said they would ask the fathers or brothers of these girls to allow this in order to help the men of Benjamin. In this way no one would actually give his daughter to a Benjamite, yet each man would have a wife. This plan worked out quite well and finally each of the 600 men of Benjamin had a wife.

The Lord Jesus has taught us not to swear, Matthew 5:34-37. Here the men of Israel swore before the Lord without considering what might happen. Soon after they were sorry for what they had done and tried to get around it by some other plan.

In those days Israel had no king. The people had the Law of Moses and the priests, but they all did what they thought was the right thing to do. Often this was wrong in the eyes of the Lord. Later Israel was ruled by kings, some of whom were good and some wicked.

God has given us the whole Bible to show us what we should do. We can also look forward to the day when the Lord Jesus Christ will rule as King over the whole earth. What a wonderful day that will be!

TEST YOURSELF (Judges 17-21)

1. What did people do when there was no king in Israel?

2. Name three sins of Micah.

3. Why did the tribe of Dan want more land?

4. Why did the Levite leave Micah?

5. Why did the second Levite go back to Bethlehem in Judah?

6. In what way were the men of Gibeah like the men of Sodom?

7. Why did the Levite cut up the dead woman into twelve pieces?

8. Who lost more men in the battle, Benjamin or the other eleven tribes?

9. Why did the tribes of Israel want to get wives for the 600 men of Benjamin who still lived?

10. What should Christians do to people who continue to sin?

Turn to page 117 to check your answers.

11 STUDIES IN RUTH

RUTH'S CHOICE, chapter 1

6/14   In the times of the judges Israel had no king. The people followed Jehovah when they had a good judge who ruled well, but many of them went back into sin when the judge died.

In Judges 17-21 we saw something of the terrible condition of the nation or part of the nation at certain times. However there were always some who wanted to follow Jehovah. In the book of Ruth we see some of these and we find God preparing the way for Israel to have a king.

The Jewish people have five little books which they read on special days at different times through the year. The book of Ruth is one of them. The others are the Song of Solomon, Lamentations, Ecclesiastes, and Esther. Ruth is read on the day of Pentecost.

Elimelech and his family lived in Bethlehem where some very wicked things happened, Judges 17:7 and 19:1. Now there was great famine in Bethlehem and Elimelech took his wife and their two sons to the land of Moab so they could get enough food to eat. God had promised to bring Israel to a land where there was plenty of everything, Joshua 5:6, but He had also warned His people that He would give them no rain if they did not obey His commands, Deuteronomy 11:16,17.

Years before this, Abraham left the land of promise in time of famine and went down to Egypt, but he got into great trouble there, Genesis 12:10-20. No doubt Elimelech knew about this and should have learned a lesson from it. Many people remained in Bethlehem, accepted God's punishment, and lived through the time of famine. Not so Elimelech. He was afraid he would die of hunger and went to Moab where the people worshiped the god Chemosh, 1 Kings 11:33. Elimelech never got back to Bethlehem but he died in the land of Moab, and so did his two sons.

Sometimes we experience real trouble and we should ask ourselves if this trouble has been sent to us by our loving Father for a reason. If this is the case we should accept it from Him and not try to run away from it, Hebrews 12:5-11.

6/15   So we have three widows in the land of Moab, Naomi, Ruth, and Orpah. Naomi, Elimelech's wife, decided to go back to Bethlehem when she heard that the famine was over, and Orpah and Ruth went with her for part of the way. At last Naomi told them to go back home to the land of Moab, and she asked the Lord to be kind to them and to give each of them another husband and a home. At first both the women said they wanted to go on to Bethlehem with Naomi. But Naomi knew that she would not give birth to any more sons who would be able to take the wives of their dead brothers as the Lord had commanded in Deuteronomy 25:5,6. Finally Orpah kissed Naomi goodbye but Ruth refused to leave her mother-in-law, 1:6-14.

6/16   Naomi reminded Ruth that Orpah had gone back to her people and her gods. But Ruth had faith in God and did not want to go back home. She told Naomi that she would go with her and live with her among the people of Israel. She wanted Jehovah to be her God and after death she wanted to be with Naomi, 1:15-18. These beautiful verses show clearly that Ruth indeed had true faith in Jehovah.

Finally the two women arrived in Bethlehem at the beginning of the harvest. The people were very surprised to see Naomi again after ten years and said, _Is this Naomi?_ The word _Naomi_ means _pleasant_, but Naomi did not think that life had been pleasant because she had lost her husband and her two sons. So she told the people to call her _Mara_ which means _bitter_ because, she said, the Lord had dealt bitterly with her. Even so her words in verse 21 seem to show that she realized that she had sinned and deserved to be punished by the Lord. She called the Lord _Almighty_, a wonderful name meaning that He takes care of His people, Genesis 17:1; 28:3. Naomi could at least have thanked God for bringing her home again.

How important it is for us to make the right decisions in life! Orpah had heard about the Lord from Naomi just as Ruth had. At first she seemed to want to go to Israel also, but then she wept and kissed Naomi and went back home to worship the gods of her people. We read nothing more about Orpah in the Bible.

No doubt it was difficult for Ruth to leave her family and home, but she made the right choice. She wanted to follow the Lord and we shall see that she was greatly blessed as a result. Like Mary she chose the right thing, Luke 10:42, and she was never sorry for it. We should ask the Lord to show us His will in all choices and decisions we have to make.

RUTH AND BOAZ, chapter 2

6/17   In this chapter we read about Boaz for the first time. Boaz was a wealthy man who belonged to the family of Elimelech and was a son of Rahab of Jericho, Matthew 1:5.

The people of Israel were commanded to remember the poor and foreigners, Leviticus 19:9,10; 23:22. Poor people were allowed to come to a field to pick up any grain left by the reapers after they had finished harvesting the field. Ruth went out to see if she could find someone kind enough to let her pick up a little grain after the reapers. She came to the field belonging to Boaz without knowing whose field it was, and she asked the man in charge if she could gather some grain. Later Boaz came and asked about Ruth and the man in charge told him who she was, 2:1-7.

6/18   Boaz allowed Ruth to stay in his field. When she was thirsty she could drink the water which his servants had brought. Ruth knew that she was only a foreigner and so she was very thankful that Boaz was kind to her, 2:10. Boaz knew that Ruth had left her own country so that she might live with the people of God and he asked the Lord to bless her, 2:11,12. Again Ruth thanked Boaz for his kindness to her, 2:13.

At mealtime Boaz told Ruth to eat with the others. He gave her more food than she could eat, 2:14. Boaz also told his servants to leave some grain on the ground on purpose so that Ruth would be able to gather it, 2:16.

6/19   Late that afternoon, Ruth began to beat out what she had gathered and she filled a whole basket with grain. She brought the grain to Naomi as well as the food she was not able to finish at noon. Naomi was pleased to hear that Ruth had been working in the field of Boaz and she explained to Ruth that Boaz belonged to their family. She told Ruth to continue to work in the same field until the harvest was over, 2:22,23.

This chapter shows us that Boaz was a spiritual man. He spoke to his servants in the name of the Lord when he came to the field and they answered him in the same way. Boaz wanted to help the poor as the Law commanded. He was very kind to Ruth and did for her much more than what the Law required. Ruth "happened" to come to Boaz' field, but we can be sure that the Lord was guiding in this also. Naomi had said before that God had dealt bitterly with her, 1:20, but now even she admitted that He had kept His promise to both those who were alive and those who had died, 2:20.

THE REDEEMER, chapter 3

6/20   Together with this chapter we should read Deuteronomy 25:5-10 as these verses will help us to understand it better. When a man died without leaving a son, his brother was expected to take his wife. The son of the dead man's wife would then be called by the name of her first husband. In this way the dead man's family would not die out. However the brother could refuse before the elders of the city to take the dead man's wife if he did not want to marry her.

Naomi's husband Elimelech had died and Naomi could have asked Boaz to act as her redeemer, but she was too old to marry again, 1:12. So she suggested that Ruth should go to Boaz instead of her. That night Boaz was winnowing his grain in the light evening wind. He slept beside the grain all night so that no one would steal it. Naomi told Ruth to see where Boaz lay down to sleep and to go and lie down at his feet a little later. This was one of the customs of the people at that time and Ruth agreed to do all that Naomi had said, 3:1-5.

6/21   Boaz woke up in the middle of the night and was surprised to find a woman at his feet. Ruth told him who she was and that he was a near relative, her *next-of-kin*. By saying this she was asking him to act as redeemer toward her according to the law of Deuteronomy 25. Boaz was glad to know that it was Ruth and blessed her in the name of the Lord. He promised to do what she requested because everyone knew she was a woman of good character. However Elimelech had another relative who had the right to take Ruth if he wanted to. Boaz said that he would find out the next day if this man was interested in marrying her, 3:6-13. In the

6/22 meantime Boaz did not want this man or anyone else to know that Ruth had been with him. The next morning he gave her six measures of grain to take back to Naomi while it was still dark. Naomi was sure that Boaz would settle the matter that very day, 3:14-18.

Here again we see that Ruth knew the Law and was willing to obey it, as did Naomi and Boaz. Let us say to our Lord as Ruth did in verse 5, *I will do whatever you tell me*, Joshua 1:16; John 2:5.

RUTH AND BOAZ ARE MARRIED, chapter 4

6/23 God did not want His people to be without any land. A person might become poor and have to sell his piece of land, but God commanded that anyone in this man's family could buy it again. In this way the land would stay in the family, Leviticus 25:25. Naomi and Boaz were also thinking of this law.

Many centuries ago cities were surrounded by great walls to keep out the enemy. People could get into the city only through the gate. Boaz went to the gate of the city of Bethlehem and soon the other near relative came along. Boaz asked ten of the elders of the city to sit down with them as witnesses. Then he told the relative that Naomi had to sell the land which belonged to her husband, and the man agreed to buy it. Then Boaz told him that he would have to take Ruth for his wife together with the field. The relative did not want to do this, so he told Boaz he could have both the land and Ruth, 4:5,6.

6/24 The relative wanted the land but he did not want to marry Ruth, the young woman from Moab. Indeed the Law taught that a Moabite could not enter the nation of Israel, Deuteronomy 23:3. The Law also teaches that we as sinners can never enter the presence of God, but we can praise God that His grace is greater than the Law, John 1:17; Romans 6:14. Boaz knew more about the grace of God than the relative. Boaz' own mother was a Canaanite, Rahab of Jericho, Matthew 1:5, and he was very glad that the relative decided he did not want Ruth.

6/25 All this business had to be done in an orderly way before the elders of the city. In those days it was the custom of men to take off their shoes to show that they agreed. Boaz called on the people who were there to witness this agreement. He bought the land from Naomi and took Ruth to be his wife. The people were glad to witness this and asked the Lord to bless Ruth and Boaz. Rachel and Leah were the wives of Jacob, and Tamar was the wife of Judah, Genesis 29:23,29; 38:6-26.

Naomi was very happy when Boaz and Ruth had a little baby boy. The women called the baby's name Obed and told Naomi that Ruth's son would look after her when she was old, 4:13-17.

Perez was the son of Judah and Tamar. The names of Perez' descendants as far as David are in verses 18 to 22. These are the same as in Matthew 1:3-6.

In this little book we read mostly about three people, Naomi, Ruth, and Boaz. The first chapter tells us about Naomi and Ruth. In the second chapter we read about Boaz for the first time and find Ruth working in the fields of Boaz. In the third chapter Ruth went to see if Boaz would marry her as the Law required. In chapter 4 we read mostly about Boaz and only a little about Naomi and Ruth. Boaz is a picture of the Lord Jesus Christ and He should become more and more important in our lives every day, John 3:30.

We can see each of these three people grow spiritually in this book. Naomi felt very bitter when she came home from Moab because she had lost her husband there and both her sons. At the end of the book we see her full of joy and thankfulness enjoying the blessing of the Lord in the home of Boaz and Ruth.

Ruth took a great step of faith when she decided to leave her home in Moab to follow the Lord God of Israel. She had a real desire to obey the Law of the Lord and in the last chapter she became the wife of Boaz.

Boaz was kind to the poor and to foreigners. He also tried to obey all the laws of God. However he knew that grace is greater than law and so he was willing to take Ruth to be his wife.

There are many lessons for us in this book.

1) We should not complain about what God allows to happen

to us knowing that He has a perfect plan for our lives and that all these things are for our good and blessing, Philippians 1:6; Romans 8:28.

2) We should always be ready to follow the Lord no matter what it may cost us. We know true blessing only when we obey His commands. Ruth became the mother of Obed, the grandfather of David the king. Many years later the Lord Jesus Christ Himself was born from the line of David. The Lord Jesus is our Redeemer and will be the King of the whole world.

TEST YOURSELF (Ruth 1-4)

1. Why did Naomi return to the land of Israel?

2. Why did Ruth return with Naomi?

3. Why did Naomi tell the people to call her Mara?

4. Why did Boaz tell his servants to drop some of the grain in the field?

5. Why was it important that Boaz was a relative of Naomi?

6. Why did Ruth go to Boaz' farm at night?

7. What did Boaz tell her?

8. Why did Boaz go into the gateway of the town?

9. Who was David's great grandmother?
   Who was his grandfather's grandmother?

10. Name the three main characters in this book and state which of them grew spiritually.

Turn to page 118 to check your answers.

12 THE TEACHING OF JUDGES AND RUTH

6/26   *It is necessary to think if you wish to learn. This part of your book will help you to learn what Judges and Ruth teach about God, about Christ, and about our salvation. Here is how you do it.*

Take a card or a piece of paper and cover all this page except the part you are reading now. Move the card down slowly a little at a time, so you can read some more. After Frame 1 you will see a question. Think about this question and try to answer it, then move your card down until you can read the answer. If you have the right answer, go on to the next paragraph. If your answer was wrong, go back and read again the whole paragraph, then try again.

THE BIBLE

1   Man is great and wonderful: he can know God through the Bible. All that we know about God comes from the Bible. Has God spoken to us in the Bible? If so, we can be sure that we have the truth about God.

The book of Judges teaches that God spoke through Moses, 1:20; 3:4. In Judges the people knew the Law came from God. Why then were they in trouble?_____

_____

– –

1. Because they did not obey God.

2   The writers of other books in the Bible believed that Judges was part of God's Word. Paul believed that God raised up the judges, Acts 13:20; Judges 2:16.

The sons of Perez are listed in Ruth 4:18-22. These names are found again in 1 Chronicles 2:5-15; Matthew 1:3-6; and Luke 3:31-33.

Name two Bible writers who believed Ruth contains the truth._____

---

2. Matthew and Luke

6/27   *GOD*

3 In the book of Judges, we read of God's wonderful works, 6:21; 13:19. Men of faith were able to do great things in the power of God, for example, Samson, 14:6; 16:30.

Name two men whose sacrifices were burned up by an act of God._____

---

3. Gideon, 6:21; Manoah, 13:19

4 Many times in Judges, God brought the people back to Himself when they had fallen into sin. He raised up judges to lead them, and gave the judges victory over their enemies. All these things show the power of God in a wonderful way.

God knew when His people went into sin. He knew when they were ready to come back to Him. He also knew the right man and called him to lead His people back to Himself, and save them from their enemies.

We can say that God knows_____. (Fill in the missing word.)

---

4. everything

5 Many verses in Judges and Ruth teach us that God is righteous. The angel of the Lord told the people of Israel that God would punish them because they did not obey His commands. Israel broke the covenant and so God in righteousness refused to drive out their enemies, 2:1-3. You can see that God is _____.

---

5. righteous

6 This same chapter in Judges tells us of the anger of Jehovah, 2:12,14,20; see also 3:8; 10:7. God's anger against His people is seen when He sent a time of famine, Ruth 1:1. Jotham believed that God would punish sin in Israel, 9:20,56,57.

On the other hand, God also punished the enemies of Israel when His people repented, 5:31. Jephthah believed that the Lord would judge righteously between Israel and the people of Ammon, 11:27. Even Adoni-Bezek, the Canaanite king, knew that he got what he deserved, 1:7.

God's anger against sin shows us that He is_____.

6/28   *6. righteous*

7 We also see the grace of God in the book of Judges. God felt sorry for the state of His people, and helped them many times, 2:18; 10:16.

Ruth was a member of the nation of Moab, but she came into the family of Israel because of her faith.

The history of Ruth shows the_____of God.

8   *7. grace*

God punished His people when they sinned, but this really shows His love to them because He wanted to draw them back to Himself. We can say God is *faithful;* this means He never changes but always does as He has promised. He fulfilled His promise to Judah, 1:2,19; to Barak, 4:14,15; to the eleven tribes, 20:28,35.

God always fulfills His promises and this teaches us that He is

                                                              8. faithful

We can be sure today that God is faithful and will take us home to be with Himself. Even God's righteousness is not against us, but for us, because Christ took our sins upon Himself. The Lord Jesus died so that God will not punish those who are in Christ. However, the Father will teach His children who do not obey His command, Hebrews 12:7,8.

This is also for our good.

CHRIST

9

What can we learn about Christ in Judges and Ruth? The Lord Jesus was born into this world in the line of David and Abraham, Matthew 1:1. In Ruth 4:18-22 we have a list of the descendants of Perez down to Boaz and David.

God had given many promises about the coming Savior. Adam and Eve knew that a man-child would gain the victory over Satan, Genesis 3:15. Abraham believed that all men would get a blessing through Him, Genesis 12:3; Galatians 3:8. God gave this promise to Isaac, Genesis 26:4; and to Jacob, 28:14. Jacob knew that the ruler would come from the tribe of Judah, Genesis 49:10, and Perez was a son of Judah, Genesis 38:29.

It is wonderful for us to know that the Son of God became man and was born into this world. God long ago knew that He would be the Son of Mary, who was a descendant of David, of the tribe of Judah.

God many times promised His people that the coming Savior would be a descendant of _____.

9. David

God also knows everything about each one of us, and wants us to do His will.

10

In Judges and Ruth, there are pictures of Christ. Samson was a Nazirite and should have lived his life separated to God. The Lord Jesus did this perfectly.

Would you say that Samson was a picture of Christ? _____

11

10. Yes, but he was a poor picture of the Lord.

The sacrifices of the Old Testament are pictures of Christ in His death. The people brought sacrifices to the Lord at Bochim, Judges 2:5. Both Gideon and Manoah brought burnt sacrifices, 6:26; 13:16,19. The eleven tribes brought burnt offerings and peace offerings, 20:26; 21:4.

What do all these offerings make you think of? _____

12 _____

11. The death of Christ.

~~Boaz was an~~ ·—·—·—·—·—·—·— ~~of our Lord Jesus Christ and also he is a~~
_____ of the Lord.

13

12. ancestor, picture

Boaz had enough money to redeem Ruth. He also had the right to do this
according to the Law, and he wanted to do it. We know that the Lord
Jesus loved us and gave His life for us in order to buy us back for
Himself. Only a near relation had the right to buy back the land of
Naomi and Ruth.

·—·—·— ~~Why did the Son of God become a Man? Hebrews 2:17;~~
4:15._____

13. So He could redeem men.

14

HOLY SPIRIT

We read about the Holy Spirit seven times in the book of Judges. He
came on Othniel who was then able to judge Israel and to overcome the
king of Aram, 3:10. The Holy Spirit came on Gideon and he called the
men of Israel to fight against the people of Midian, 6:34. The Holy Spirit
came on Jephthah and he gained a victory over the Ammonites,
11:29,32. Of Samson it is said the Holy Spirit *began* to stir him, 13:25.
This is the sad part of Samson's life. He followed his own desires and
the Holy Spirit could not use him fully. However, the Holy Spirit made
Samson strong enough to kill a lion, 14:6; thirty Philistines, 14:19; and
another time, a thousand Philistines, 15:14,15.

·—·—·— ~~How can we overcome our enemies?~~ ·—·—·—·—·—·—·—·—
_____

14. The Holy Spirit will help us.

15

SIN

Soon after Joshua died, the people of Israel began to fall into great sin. The first of the Ten Commandments says that we should have no other gods beside the Lord. The second Commandment tells us not to make an image or to bow down before any image, Exodus 20:3-5. In Judges, we see the people of Israel following other gods, 3:6; 6:25; 8:33; 10:6. Some of them made images, 17:4; others wanted these images so badly, they stole them, 18:18. Even a descendant of Moses was willing to look after these idols and he got paid for his work, 17:10; 18:30. The last part of the book of Judges also shows us the terrible sin of the men of Benjamin, 19:25.

The people of Israel often broke the first Commandment by worshiping a false god called_____.

16

15. Baal

Even the leaders of Israel were guilty of sin. Read 8:27; 9:5; 16:1,4.

Who made an ephod?_____

Who killed his brothers?_____

Who loved women of the world?_____.

6/30

17   *16. Gideon, Abimelech, Samson*

FAITH

Without faith, it is not possible for anyone to please God. In Judges and Ruth, we see many examples of true faith. God is always willing to help His people when they turn to Him in faith. The judges of Israel all had faith when they delivered the people of Israel from their enemies. Some had only a little faith and God helped them. These books, Judges and Ruth, teach us that we should_____
_____ in God.

18

17. believe or have faith

For example, Gideon saw the power of God, 6:21. Then the Lord told him to do a hard thing — to pull down the altar of Baal, 6:25. Gideon did it, but at night. We may say he had faith, but not great faith. Even after the Spirit of God came upon him, he asked the Lord for a special sign, 6:36-40. Then the Lord told him to do another hard thing, to send home most of the men, 7:2-8. Then the Lord gave him still another sign, 7:9-14.

Each time God showed Gideon His_____, Gideon acted in _____.

19

18. power, faith

Often we think we have only a little faith. We can be sure that the Lord will_____us, Mark 9:24, and we can do_____things for Him with only a little faith, Matthew 17:20.

20

19. help, great

Ruth is the great example of faith in these books. Naomi told her about Jehovah and Ruth believed, Ruth 1:16,17; 2:12.

Ruth showed her faith by leaving_____and going to _____.

21

20. Moab, Israel

In the book of Judges faith brought victory. Sometimes it was only partial victory and Israel did not drive out their enemies, 1:28,29,30. When God saw true faith, He made His servants brave, for example, Ehud, 3:20-23.

Name three women in the book of Judges who had real faith, 4:4,21; 13:3._____

21. Deborah, Jael, the wife of Manoah

22

THE LAST THINGS

Many books in the Bible tell us what God is going to do in the last days but we do not find teaching on these things in the book of Judges. We do read that there was no _____in Israel in those days, 17:6; 18:1; 19:1; 21:25. For the future, God has decided that Jesus Christ will_____over the whole world, Revelation 19:16.

22. king, rule

The great lesson of the book of Judges is that God's people must obey His Word if they want blessing and victory. If we do not obey, God will send trouble. Anyone who has faith should be ready for the Lord to use him to help His people. Even so, there will never be full blessing in this world until the Lord Jesus Christ, the rightful King, comes back to rule. Are you ready to meet Him?

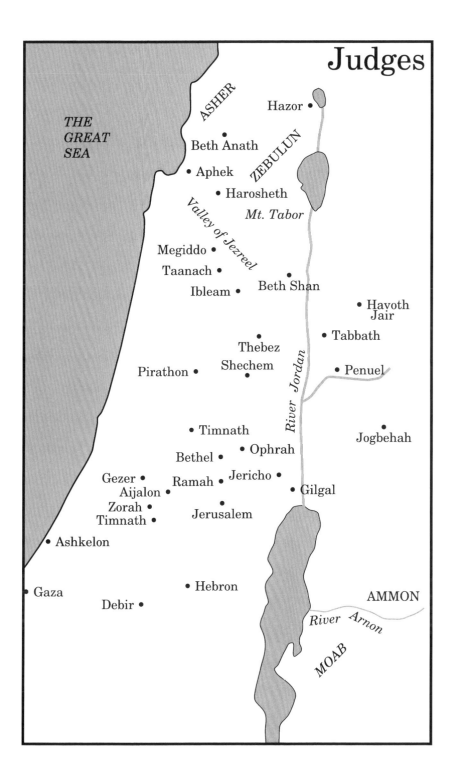

Answers to *Test Yourself*

JOSHUA 1-4

1. They were slaves in Egypt until God sent Moses to deliver them and to lead them through the desert to the land which God had promised to them.

2. Egypt, Ephraim.

3. That victory comes through prayer.

4. Moses had died and enemies occupied the land which God had promised to Israel. God told Joshua to be brave and obey His commands.

5. They had a lot of cattle and were more interested in their wealth than in the Lord.

6. She helped God's people and wanted to save her own family.

7. She thought this was the only way to save the two men of Israel. The Bible tells us that it is wrong to tell lies.

8. Because God was going to do a great miracle and help them to enter the land of Canaan.

9. Only when the priests' feet were actually in the water.

10. To remind people in the future that God had helped them to enter their land.

11. Only 40,000 men crossed the Jordan River to help.

JOSHUA 5-8

1. The circumcision was a sign of God's covenant with Israel. It was necessary before they could expect God's blessing.

2. The Passover Lamb speaks of our Lord Jesus Christ who was killed for us.

3. God was their Captain and Joshua worshiped Him, 5:14.

4. 1) Rahab and her family.
   2) Everything made of metal.
   3) Achan saved a beautiful piece of clothing.

5. She married Salmon and became an ancestor of the Lord Jesus as a Man.

6. God was not with them because one of them had committed sin.

7. Yes, but only after he was found out. This was not true repentance and he had to die for his sin.

8. Achan and his family, also 36 men of Israel, 7:5,24.

9. The whole army but he sent some of them to hide behind the city, 8:11,12.

10. First he set up an altar and offered sacrifices; then he wrote down the Law of Moses and read it to the people.

JOSHUA 9-12

1. They heard of Israel's victories and were afraid they would be killed.

2. He and the chief men did not first ask the Lord to guide them, 9:14.

3. They made them slaves but did not kill them, 9:21.

4. Sometimes he uses force: six kings joined to fight against Israel, vs. 1,2. Sometimes he tries to deceive us: the Gibeonites told Israel a lie.

5. The Gibeonites had agreed to be slaves of Israel.

6. 1) He made the Amorites afraid, 10:10.
   2) He threw great hail stones on them, 10:11.
   3) He made the daylight last much longer so Joshua's army could gain a complete victory.

7. Yes. God created the world and He could slow it down so that it turned slowly on its axis. This made the daylight last much longer.

8. It was a sign of complete victory and helped them to believe that they would be able to defeat the other kings of Canaan.

9. One was a friend of God's servant Abraham, and the other was an enemy of God's servant Joshua.

10. They joined together to fight against Israel so Joshua was able,

with God's help, to destroy them all at once.

JOSHUA 13-21

1.   Reubenites, Gadites, and half the tribe of Manasseh.

2.   Balaam led Israel into sin and lived with their enemies so he had to die with them also.

3.   He wanted to fight the battles of the Lord and he asked for country where giants lived.

4.   Othniel proved that he could trust the Lord and win battles in His name.

5.   Jerusalem was in Judah's territory but the city was given to the tribe of Benjamin, 15:8,63; 18:28.

6.   They said they needed more land but they had not yet conquered all the land they had been given.

7.   Shiloh was the capital city of Israel and Joshua called them there to divide up the rest of the land.

8.   Timnath-Serah in the land of Ephraim.

9.   There were six cities of refuge where a man could run and be safe if he killed someone but had not planned to do it.

10. The Levites did not require farms because the other tribes gave them food and money so they could serve the Lord. However, the Levites received 48 cities and enough land around each city for the Levites' animals.

JUDGES 1-3

1.   In Joshua we read of Israel's many victories and a few failures. In Judges we read of Israel's many failures and a few victories.

2.   1) Israel continued to fight for their land but often failed.
     2) God raised up 14 judges to deliver His people.
     3) The people of Israel fell into terrible sin because every man did what he pleased, 21:25.

3.   Adoni-Bezek had done the same to 70 kings and he knew he

deserved the same. But God had commanded Israel to destroy the wicked people of Canaan so the men of Judah should not have allowed him to live.

4. God was happy to see the faith of these young people.

5. Manasseh, v.27; Ephraim, v.29; Zebulun, v.30; Asher, v.31; Naphtali, v.33; Dan, v.34.

6. An angel of Jehovah told the men of Israel they had sinned and so God did not give them victory. The people wept and offered sacrifices to God.

7. 1) He showed the people God's Law and brought them back to the Lord.
   2) Then he led them in battle and God delivered them from their enemies.

8. Idolatry. God commanded Israel to destroy the nations of Canaan because they worshiped idols. Yet Israel fell into the same terrible sin again and again.

9. Ehud knew God would judge Eglon and deliver His people Israel. Ehud brought this message when he bravely killed the fat and wicked king in his own palace.

10. We believers have great and powerful enemies: the world, the flesh, and the devil. Only the Lord Jesus can save us from these enemies.

JUDGES 4-8

1. They must confess their sins and put them away.

2. Deborah was not speaking about herself. Jael was a brave woman who killed the enemy of God's people.

3. Miriam, Exodus 15:21, and Deborah, Judges 5:1.

4. So the wicked Midianites would not see him and steal the grain.

5. Because he had destroyed the altar of the false god whom they worshiped.

6. He wanted everyone to know that He alone would give the victory and the glory should be His.

7. 1) He sent fire to burn up Gideon's sacrifice, 6:21.
   2) He made the sheep skin wet one night and dry the next, 6:38,40.
   3) He gave a dream to one of the soldiers of Midian, 7:13-15.

8. They saw 300 lamps and heard 300 trumpets so they thought they were surrounded by a great army. They lost control of themselves and the Lord set them fighting against each other.

9. He answered them softly and they were no longer angry.

10. He made an ephod like the one used only by the priests of Israel, 8:27.

JUDGES 9-12

1. He was a brave soldier but a wicked man.

2. There were seventy sons and all were killed by Abimelech except one, Jotham.

3. Because the men of Shechem had chosen a wicked man to be their king. They were like the trees which chose the bramble because no other tree would rule over them.

4. A woman threw a large stone on his head, so he asked his helper to kill him quickly.

5. Israel had rejected Jehovah and served these false gods. Now they were in trouble but God refused to help them until they really repented, v.16.

6. His family had rejected him because of his mother. Then the men of Gilead agreed that he would be their leader if he led them in the battle.

7. He tried to persuade him that Ammon did not have any right to claim the land of Gilead.

8. He had promised to give to Jehovah the first one that met him when he returned home after his victory.

9. Gideon spoke quietly to the jealous men of Ephraim, but Jephthah fought with them.

10.   To find out if they were men of Ephraim. The people of Ephraim spoke a little differently and anyone could tell they belonged to Ephraim.

JUDGES 13-16

1.   A man who decided to set aside part of his life for the work of the Lord.

2.   He promised she would have a son who would be a Nazirite from the time he was born. Nazirites could not drink wine so the mother should not.

3.   He was sure that God Himself had spoken to him and his wife and he knew that he was a sinner.

4.   They both knew that God had called them to deliver His people and they both chose the wrong way.

5.   He was a Nazirite and he should not have touched a dead body.

6.   Samson was angry because his wife had been given to another man. The foxes set fire to the crops of the Philistines.

7.   They were afraid of the Philistines and did not believe in God.

8.   She wanted the 5,500 pieces of silver which the lords of the Philistines had promised her.

9.   Samson was strong only when the Lord was with him.

10.   Samson was strong sometimes and weak at other times. He tried to be spiritual and yet he loved the world. So in Laodicea. The Lord said the Christians there were neither cold nor hot, Revelation 3:15. They were half and half. Let us be altogether for the Lord and   give ourselves wholly to Him!

JUDGES 17-21

1.   Every man did what he thought was right, but this was often sinful.

2.   1) He stole his mother's money, 17:2.

   2) He made a house for his images, 17:5.

   3) He made his son a priest, then he hired a Levite and made him his priest, 17:5,10-12.

3. They were not able to drive the Amorites out of the land which God had given them.

4. He thought he would get more money acting as a priest for a large family and not just for one man.

5. His woman had run away from him and gone back to her father in Bethlehem.

6. They wanted to commit sin with a man, a visitor.

7. The men of Gibeah had killed her and the Levite wanted all the tribes of Israel to know about this terrible sin.

8. Benjamin had 26,700 men, 20:15, and they all died, except 600, but first they destroyed 40,030 men from Judah and the other tribes, 20:21,25,39.

9. They did not want one of the twelve tribes to be completely destroyed.

10. They should be put out of the church until they repent and confess their sins.

RUTH 1-4

1. She heard that the famine was over, 1:6.

2. She had learned to love the Lord God of Israel, 1:16.

3. Mara means *bitter* and she thought that God had been unkind to her because her husband and her two sons had died in Moab.

4. He wanted to help Ruth who had come to pick up the grain which the servants left.

5. Naomi had to sell the family property and any near relative could buy it, Leviticus 25:25.

6. She wanted to tell him privately that she was a near relative and to ask him if he would take care of her, 3:9.

7. He said he would be glad to have her but there was another man who could have her if he wanted because he was nearer than Boaz to Elimelech's family.

JUDGES OF ISRAEL

Oppressor	Gentile Nation	Years of Oppression	Judge	Tribe	Said to be Savior	Said to be Judge	Used by Holy Spirit	Years of Peace	Chapter
Cushan-Rishathaim	Mesopotamia	8	Othniel	Judah	3:9	3:10	3:10	40	3:8-11
Eglon	Moab	18	Ehud	Benjamin	3:15			80	3:13-20
	Philistines		Shamgar		3:31				3:31
Jabin / Sisera	Canaan	20	Deborah / Barak	Napthali		4:4		40	4:1-5:31
	Midian	7	Gideon	Manasseh	6:14		6:34	40	6:1-8:35
			Abimelech	Manasseh					9:1-57
			Tola	Issachar	10:1	10:2		23	10:1,2
			Jair	Manasseh		10:3		22	10:3-5
	Ammonites	18	Jephthah	Manasseh		12:7	11:29	6	10:6-11:40
			Ibzan	Judah		12:8		7	12:8-10
			Elon	Zebulun		12:11		10	12:11-12
			Abdon	Ephraim		12:13		8	12:13-15
	Philistines	40	Samson	Dan	13:5	15:20	13:25;14:6,19 15:14	20	13:1-16:31